P9-CLB-205

DATE DUE

Brodart Co.   Cat. # 55 137 001   Printed in USA

CULTURES OF THE WORLD
Mexico

Marshall Cavendish
Benchmark

New York

PICTURE CREDITS
Cover: © Stock Connection / SuperStock
Corbis/Click Photos: 35 • Getty Images: 37 • Inmagine.com: 3, 6, 13, 15, 16, 18, 20, 22, 23, 25, 26, 32, 43, 44, 57, 58, 59, 60, 61, 64, 65, 66, 67, 68, 69, 70, 71, 72, 80, 96, 97, 99, 100, 104, 109, 110, 114, 122, 124, 125, 131 • Marshall Cavendish Archives: 88, 89, 126, 127, 130 • Photolibrary: 1, 5, 8, 10, 11, 12, 24, 27, 29, 33, 34, 38, 39, 40, 41, 42, 46, 50, 51, 52, 53, 56, 73, 74, 75, 76, 78, 79, 82, 84, 85, 86, 90, 91, 92, 93, 94, 95, 98, 101, 102, 105, 106, 107, 108, 112, 113, 115, 118, 120, 121, 123

PRECEDING PAGE
Children dressed up in traditional Mexican wear.

Publisher (U.S.): Michelle Bisson
Writers: Mary Jo Reilly, Leslie Jermyn, Michael Spilling
Editors: Deborah Grahame-Smith, Mindy Pang
Copyreader: Sherry Chiger
Designers: Nancy Sabato, Bernard Go
Cover picture researcher: Tracey Engel
Picture researcher: Joshua Ang

Marshall Cavendish Benchmark
99 White Plains Road
Tarrytown, NY 10591
Website: www.marshallcavendish.us

Originated and designed by Times Media Private Limited
An imprint of Marshall Cavendish International (Asia) Private Limited
A member of Times Publishing Limited

Marshall Cavendish is a trademark of Times Publishing Limited.

Library of Congress Cataloging-in-Publication Data
Reilly, Mary Jo, 1964–.
  Mexico / by Mary Jo Reilly, Leslie Jermyn, and Michael Spilling. — 3rd ed.
    p. cm. — (Cultures of the world)
  Includes bibliographical references and index.
  Summary: "Provides comprehensive information on the geography, history, wildlife, governmental structure, economy, cultural diversity, peoples, religion, and culture of Mexico"—Provided by publisher.
  ISBN 978-1-60870-802-4 (print) — ISBN 978-1-60870-809-3 (ebook)
  1. Mexico—Juvenile literature. I. Jermyn, Leslie. II. Spilling, Michael.
III. Title. IV. Series.

  F1208.5.R45 2012
  972—dc23   2011025244

Printed in Malaysia
7 6 5 4 3 2 1

CONTENTS

MEXICO TODAY

MEXICO IS ONE OF THE MOST CULTURALLY DIVERSE COUNTRIES in the world. It combines a patchwork of Native American cultures with traditions developed by the Spanish during three centuries of colonial rule. Regional identities are still very strong in Mexico, giving the country a dynamism all its own. The Spanish invasion of Mexico in 1521 was, at the time, the greatest military expedition in history. Mexico then languished as a Spanish colony for more than 300 years and was basically a feudal country. Mexicans today reflect a blend of local Native American culture and Spanish colonial rule.

The nation of Mexico, with its current borders, has existed only for around 150 years. Mexico as a political entity can be traced to the Spanish conquest and the following period of colonial development. Before the arrival of the Spanish, Mexico was home to various native cultures extending from what is today the southwestern United States and down through Mexico into Central America. These Mesoamerican civilizations included the Mayans, the Olmecs, the Aztecs, the Toltecs, the Teotihuacáns, the Huastecs, the Veracruz, and the Mixtecs. These ancient native cultures are still apparent today in some of the most spectacular and architecturally

Mexican women dressed in Aztec costumes.

impressive ruins on the North American continent. Locals and tourists alike flock to see the statue-topped pyramids at Tula, the Mayan murals at Bonampak, the Mayan temples at Palenque, and the spectacular complex at Chichén Itzá.

Most Mexicans are of mestizo ancestry, being a mixture of both Indian and Spanish blood. A few pure indigenous Indian communities remain, and even fewer Mexicans of pure Spanish or European descent. Mexico's indigenous population numbers more than 10 million people and is concentrated in the southern and south-central regions of Mexico. The principal groups are the Náhuatls, the Mayans, the Zapotecs, the Mixtecs, and the Otomis. The indigenous population constitutes 11 percent of the total population. These groups each number in the hundreds of thousands, if not millions, but there are also small ethnic groups, such as the Cochimíes, the Ixils, and the Kaqchikels, which number just a few hundred people. Although Spanish is spoken by almost everyone, it is not the only recognized official language, as 62 indigenous languages have also been given status as national languages. Náhuatl is spoken by 1.6 million people, whereas others, such as Aguacatec, are spoken by just a few families!

Mexico has many points of connectedness, both cultural and economic, with its more powerful northern neighbor, the United States. Despite the influence of the United States, however, Mexico retains a very distinct identity. Mexicans have their own way of doing things, with festivals, food, language, and an artistic culture that are uniquely their own. The music that fills the town and city squares in the evening is Mexican, the popular television shows—especially the soaps—are Mexican, and the food sold by street hawkers and in local restaurants have a strong and recognizable local flavor. In fact, many of the world's favorite ingredients originate from Mexico, including cacao (for making chocolate), tomato, corn, avocado, vanilla, and jalapeño peppers.

While the United States remains Mexico's most important trading partner, and millions of Mexicans live and work in the United States, life in Mexico remains distinct and separate from that of its northern neighbor.

While traditionally most Mexicans lived rural lives based on farming, today around 75 percent of the population live in cities. Roughly a third of all Mexicans live in the three main cities: Mexico City (the capital), Guadalajara, and Monterrey. Mexico's cities reflect the cultural and historical diversity of the country as a whole: In a city such as Monterrey, you might see Mayan traders selling traditional wares on a street corner while on the next block teenage boys play soccer in front of a Spanish colonial church.

The family is the center of all social life in Mexico, and extended families still live together. Many households are home to at least three generations of the same family, and it is common for up to 10 people to live under one roof. Although more women have taken up professional careers in recent decades, it is still traditional for the mother to stay at home and care for the house and the family. On weekends people will shop and eat in the lively, colorful markets, or if they live in a city, they might visit a mall to browse, eat, and shop.

Sports are very important for Mexicans, especially the men. Rodeo, soccer, and bullfighting are some of the popular pastimes and spectator activities. Soccer especially draws in crowds of millions every weekend, when the major teams play against each other. Watching one of the capital's big teams, such as Club América or Atlante, playing at Mexico City's 120,000-seat Estadio Azteca (Aztec Stadium), the site of the 1970 and 1986 World Cup soccer finals, is one of the great Mexican cultural experiences.

The fiesta, or festival, is also a key part of Mexican life. From the remotest villages to the largest cities, every part of Mexico has its own festival where people devote at least a day to celebrating. In most cases it is to mark a local saint's day, but some fiestas have pre-Christian origins, marking the beginning of the rainy season or the end of the harvest. Carnaval, the Catholic festival to mark the beginning of Lent, is celebrated throughout Mexico for five days. Mexicans go out into the streets and parade in costumes, dance, eat, and drink. The festival climaxes on the final day, called Mardi Gras. Semana Santa, or Holy Week, is Mexico's second most important holiday season of the year, behind only Christmas. Mexico is nearly 90 percent Catholic, and the entire

A woman selling vegetables at a market stand in Oaxaca.

community shares and participates in this festival. Semana Santa ends the 40-day Lent period and includes Good Friday and Easter Sunday. Mexicans worship the Virgin Mary with processions carrying statues and images through the streets of every village, town, and city.

With its growing manufacturing sector, Mexico has developed into a big economic player and is ranked the 13th largest economy in the world today. Mexico's proximity to and relationship with the United States have brought many benefits, especially economic. Since the declaration of the North American Free Trade Agreement (NAFTA) in 1994, the Mexican economy has bloomed, and the United States remains Mexico's largest trading partner and the biggest market for Mexican goods and services. Successful growth has been led by a strong export-based approach: Mexico has negotiated free-trade agreements with 50 other countries around the world, accounting for 90 percent of its annual wealth creation.

However, while Mexico's flourishing economy has helped create wealth throughout the country, the extremes of wealth and poverty can be seen everywhere. In the big cities large numbers of people live in unhealthy and overcrowded slums. Yet just a few miles away wealthy districts are home to huge mansions with expensive cars and servants. The poorest 10 percent of households share less than 2 percent of the country's wealth, whereas the top 10 percent have 42 percent of the country's wealth. These vast disparities are something the Mexican government has tried to address through better schooling, improved labor laws, and most important, job creation.

Most Mexicans work in factories that produce electronic goods or other manufactured products, ranging from auto parts to computer hard drives. The agricultural sector has shrunk during the past 30 years to become a small part of the economy, employing just a fraction of the workforce.

It is traditional in Mexico for workers to take a siesta—a break involving lunch and sometimes a nap for a few hours in the middle of the day. Little restaurants (called *cocinas económicas*, "economical kitchens") open for a couple of hours to serve lunch for just a few dollars. Workers flock there during siesta time, when most offices and businesses close. Fresh fish, chicken, meat, and vegetables are served, along with rice, tortillas, a cold drink, and dessert. In the evenings, street vendors open up their portable food wagons after 7 P.M., serving light meals, such as pork sandwiches, hamburgers, tacos, and ears of corn, along with lots of cola, one of Mexico's most popular drinks.

Mexico's geography is as diverse as its culture. Two great mountain ranges, the Sierra Madre Occidental in the west and the Sierra Madre Oriental in the east, divide the country, running parallel along the coasts, enclosing a large, arid central plateau. In the center of the country are the volcanic highlands, upon which Mexico City sits. The country in the south and in the Yucatán Peninsula is subtropical and home to rain forests and pure sandy beaches.

Mexico is counted among the 18 "megadiverse" countries in the world, meaning that most of the world's major species live within the country's borders. With more than 200,000 species, Mexico is home to 12 percent of the world's biodiversity, including more than 700 species of reptiles alone. This huge diversity brings challenges, however, such as deforestation, often caused by thoughtless logging practices. Furthermore, many of Mexico's native species are threatened by the expansion of industries, improvements in infrastructure, and more-efficient farming methods.

In 2010 Mexicans celebrated two events that shaped modern Mexico: the 200th anniversary of national independence and the centennial of the Mexican Revolution. These celebrations gave Mexicans time to reflect on their past and look to the future.

Mexico is likely to face many challenges in the next few years, not the least how to continue to expand the economy and reduce poverty while at the same time preserving its diverse ecosystem for future generations. The government of President Felipe Calderón has set for itself the target of improving public education and upgrading the country's infrastructure to help generate more wealth, distribute it more evenly, and bring a better quality of life to all Mexicans.

GEOGRAPHY

A view of Mount Popocatépetl in Puebla. The Aztecs once worshiped the volcano as a god.

1

MEXICO IS BORDERED BY THE United States to the north, Guatemala to the south, and Belize to the southeast. Mexico's total surface area is 3,287,612 square miles (8,514,877 square km), making it the world's 14th-largest country by total area. It includes approximately 3,266,199 square miles (8,459,417 square km) of land areas and 21,413 square miles (55,460 square km) of water areas.

The Aldama sinkholes or cenotes in Tamaulipas are vertical caves filled with mineralized freshwater.

The arid desert landscape of the large Baja California region extends all the way to the turquoise waters of the La Paz Gulf.

Stretching for 2,000 miles (3,218 km) at its widest point, Mexico's shores are washed by the Pacific Ocean to the west and the Gulf of Mexico and the Caribbean Sea to the east. Slightly less than three times the size of Texas, Mexico is the third-largest Latin American country, after Brazil and Argentina.

Mexico's early civilizations occupied territory beyond the country's current borders. To the south, these early cultures reached into Guatemala, Belize, El Salvador, and Honduras; to the north, they extended about 300 miles (482 km) north of the Central Valley of Mexico City. This historical area is referred to as Mesoamerica.

GEOGRAPHICAL REGIONS

Most of Mexico's land is made up of mountains and plateaus. Two great mountain chains—the Sierra Madre Oriental and the Sierra Madre Occidental—run north to south through the country. These two chains form part of a long system of mountains that run up along the west coasts of North America, Central America, and South America. This range splits into two in Mexico. The western arm continues northward and links up with the Rocky Mountains in the United States.

Mexico has an amazingly diverse landscape, consisting of snowcapped mountains and tropical rain forests, beaches and plateaus, barren desert and fertile farmland. The country can be divided into five topographic regions based on climate, landforms, and vegetation patterns.

THE PACIFIC NORTHWEST This very dry region covers the states of Baja California Norte, Baja California Sur, and Sinola, as well as western Sonora and northern Nayarit. Baja California, an 800-mile-long (1,287-km-long) peninsula as long as Florida, is basically a desert.

With so little rain, the landscape of the Pacific northwest is dominated by desert brush and cacti. There are pockets of land where farming occurs, but the land is difficult to cultivate.

The Colorado River Delta forms a large lowland in the northeastern part of this region. As the delta grew, it cut off and dried up the northernmost and southernmost parts of the Gulf of California, forming the Imperial Valley in California and the Mexicali Valley in Mexico.

The Pacific northwest's mainland coastal strip is better for farming because it has fertile valleys irrigated by rivers, including the Colorado, the Yaqui, and the Fuerte. In addition to farmland, these basins support cattle ranches and rich copper and silver mines.

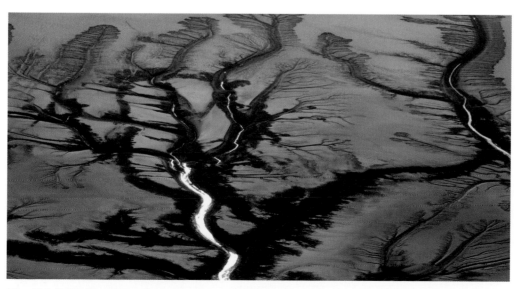

The distributaries of the Colorado River Delta stand out starkly in the Sonoran desertscape.

VOLCANOES

Mexico's most famous volcanoes are Popocatépetl (17,802 feet/5,426 m), and Iztaccíhuatl. Iztaccíhuatl has four peaks, the highest of which is 17,159 feet (5,230 m) above sea level. Popocatépetl, which means "smoking mountain" in the Náhuatl Indian language, has not erupted since 1702, but it still releases huge clouds of smoke. Iztaccíhuatl, or "sleeping woman," lies next to it. According to legend, the volcanoes are named after two lovers: Popo, a warrior, and Ixta, a princess. When Ixta died, Popo laid her body on one mountain and stood, holding her funeral torch, on the other.

Paricutín, the youngest volcano in Mexico, emerged in the Mexican state of Michoacán on February 7, 1943. It grew in the middle of a cornfield to 9,101 feet (2,774 m) in height, poured out tons of lava, and destroyed several villages. It has been dormant since 1952 but can become active again. The most active volcano in recent years is Colima, near the town of Yerbabuena. It has erupted more than 40 times since 1576. People in the area have been evacuated repeatedly since 1998 in response to indications that it would blow again. The largest eruption in recent years happened on May 24, 2005. An ash cloud rose to more than 2 miles (3.2 km) above the volcano. Satellite monitoring showed that the cloud spread over an area extending 110 miles (177 km) west of the volcano in the hours after the eruption.

THE CENTRAL PLATEAU This area is located between the two Sierra Madre chains. While the Sonora Desert lies in arid northwestern Mexico, the southern areas contain some of the richest, most fertile farmland in Mexico. Summer rains usually provide good growing conditions for small grains, such as corn and rice. The western part of the plateau also contains the manufacturing centers of Guadalajara, León, Querétaro, and San Luis Potosí.

THE GULF COASTAL PLAIN AND THE YUCATÁN The geography of the Gulf Coastal Plain and the Yucatán Peninsula changes gradually from north to south. Both regions are dry in the north, but they get wetter toward the south until they end in tropical rain forests. Wetlands along the Gulf Coast consist of numerous large complexes of fresh, brackish, and salt marshes and mangrove swamps.

The Gulf Coastal Plain is located in the states of Nuevo León, Tamaulipas, Veracruz, and Tabasco. Farming is possible in the northern part of the plain, where the soil is watered by nearby rivers. In contrast, no rivers run through the Yucatán Peninsula. This section is dominated by a limestone plateau with underground channels leading to the sea. Huge pits have formed where the roofs of these channels have fallen in. These pits were once the sacred wells of the Mayan Indians.

The Xlacah cenote in Mexico. Cenotes are part of an underground water system running through the Yucatán.

THE SIERRA VOLCÁNICA TRANSVERSAL This region forms a major geological break with the Central Plateau. Hundreds of volcanic mountains, countless cinder cones, lava flows, ash deposits, hot springs, and other remarkable landmarks tell of past and present volcanic activity.

The soil and climate of the Sierra Volcánica Transversal have made the region very attractive to settlers. It has become the most populated area of Mexico, and it includes the capital, Mexico City, and the cities of Toluca and Puebla. Unfortunately the basins in this area trap dirty air generated by the cities, making air pollution a major problem.

THE SOUTHERN UPLANDS This region is characterized by steep mountain ridges and deep gorges cut by mountain streams. Several of Mexico's most popular tourist destinations are in this region, including the famed resort city of Acapulco and Monte Albán, the ancient Indian religious center.

CLIMATE

Cactus plants are found in many parts of Mexico where the climate is usually hot and dry.

Most people think of Mexico as a hot, dry country. But Mexico has snowcapped mountains, tropical rain forests, and rich grasslands in addition to deserts. Northwestern Mexico and inland northern areas are drier than the rest of the country. It is hot in the summer, but north winds can make inland northern Mexico chilly in winter, with temperatures sometimes approaching freezing.

The Tropic of Cancer cuts Mexico almost exactly in half, putting the southern part of the country in the tropical zone and the northern part in the temperate zone. However, the climate in Mexico is determined as much by altitude as by latitude. Thus the southern tropical zone, which has a wide variety of altitudes, actually includes hot, temperate, and cool areas. Moreover, the northern temperate zone has some of the driest deserts to be found anywhere in the world.

Generally the coastal lowlands are hot, the plateaus are temperate, and the mountains are cool. Mexicans have named these temperature zones. *Tierra caliente* (tee-EH-rah cah-lee-EN-tay), or "hot land," refers to the coastal areas and lowlands. *Tierra templada* (tee-EH-rah tem-PLAH-dah), or "temperate land," includes areas from 3,000 to 6,000 feet (914—1,829 m) above sea level. *Tierra fría* (tee-EH-rah FREE-ah), or "cold land," is everything above 6,000 feet (1,829 m).

Mexico City, which lies about 7,350 feet (2,240 m) above sea level, is warm during the day and cool at night. The north and northwest of Mexico, which belong to the same desert belt as Southern California and Arizona, are very dry.

Rain falls mostly in the mountains near the coasts, leaving the interior of Mexico very dry. The eastern coast gets much more rain than the Pacific coast. Only about 12 percent of the country gets enough rainfall to support the cultivation of crops without irrigation, and almost half of the country gets approximately 29 inches (737 mm) of rain annually. Except in Baja California, most of the year's rain falls between summer and early fall. Mexico's hot and wet season lasts from May to October. December to February are the cool months.

MEXICO CITY EARTHQUAKE

On September 19, 1985, a powerful earthquake struck Mexico City, killing an estimated 10,000 people and injuring 30,000 more. It left nearly 250,000 people homeless. At 7:19 in the morning, Mexico City's residents were jolted awake by an 8.1-magnitude earthquake, one of the strongest ever to hit the area. The effects of the quake were particularly devastating to the city: Mexico City sits atop a plateau, surrounded by mountains, but that plateau was formed from a lake that had been drained over many thousands of years, leaving an unstable base of dirt and sand.

The earthquake on September 19 was centered 250 miles (402 km) west of the city. Due to the unstable ground underneath the city, however, serious shaking lasted for nearly three minutes. The prolonged ground movement caused several old buildings, including the Regis, Versailles, and Romano hotels, to crumble. Many shoddily built factory buildings were also destroyed. The tremors caused gas mains to break, causing fires and explosions throughout the city.

The seismic event was made up of four quakes in all. A pre-event quake of magnitude 5.2 occurred on May 28, 1985. The main and most powerful shock occurred on September 19, followed by two aftershocks: one on September 20, 1985, and a second seven months later, on April 30, 1986.

When the damage was finally assessed, it was found that the quake seriously affected an area of 318,450 square miles (824,782 square km) and caused up to $4 billion in damage, as more than 410 buildings collapsed and another 3,124 were seriously damaged in Mexico City.

FLORA

Enormous differences in climate naturally result in a wide variety of plant life in Mexico. The arid northern, northwestern, and central regions produce plants that are adapted to a limited water supply, such as cacti, agaves, cassavas, mesquites, and brush plants.

In the south and the east, as well as on the western coasts, rain forests, savannas, grazing land, and spiny plants dominate the landscape. Some of Mexico's mountains are snowcapped, some are forested, and others are completely barren.

Mexico is home to what is said to be the oldest living thing on the American continents: a giant ahuehuete tree that Mexicans call El Árbol del Tule, or the Tree of Tula. The tree is more than 2,000 years old and is located on the church grounds in the town of Santa María del Tule, in the Mexican state of Oaxaca. In 2005 its trunk had a circumference of more than 160 feet (48.8 m),

The poinsettia, the popular floral symbol of Christmas, is native to Mexico. The plant is usually found in moist, wet, wooded ravines and rocky hillsides.

The Árbol del Tule stands within the church grounds in the town center of Santa María del Tule in the state of Oaxaca. It has the stoutest trunk of any tree in the world and is nicknamed the "Tree of Life" because of the numerous images of animals reputedly visible on the tree's gnarled trunk.

FAUNA

Mexico has a rich diversity of animal life that includes species from both North and South America.

Birds, reptiles, insects, and a variety of mammals, including wild sheep, deer, bears, and possums, are plentiful. The tropical rain forests contain such exotic animals as monkeys, jaguars, wild boars, and cougars. The unique volcano rabbit, known as *teporingo* (teh-POH-rin-go) in Mexico, is found only around the Popocatépetl and Iztaccíhuatl volcanoes. Weighing just 14 to 21 ounces (397—595 g), it is the world's second-smallest rabbit, after the pygmy rabbit.

Marine life off the coast of Mexico is equally varied, consisting of a wealth of fish and underwater organisms. The northernmost stretch of Mexico's Pacific coast is washed by the Gulf of California, a sheltered sea that opens to the south into the Pacific Ocean. The meeting of the distinct marine environments of the Gulf and the Pacific encourages the growth of a wide variety of fish. Marlin, black sea bass, and sailfish are found far offshore, whereas smaller species such as porgy and amberjack can be seen closer to the beach.

Perhaps the most spectacular of the mammals off Mexico's coast is the gray whale, which migrates every winter to the waters off Baja California to mate and calve. Virtually extinct 60 years ago, the gray whale has made an amazing comeback. In the waters off Baja California, its favorite breeding ground, the number of whales has risen from 250 in 1937 to 26,000 in recent years.

Another previously endangered mammal that has made a remarkable recovery since the beginning of the 20th century is the elephant seal, which is found near Guadalupe Island.

INTERNET LINKS

www.plant-talk.org/mexico-in-pictures-giant-cypress-tree-tule.htm

This website provides good photographs of the huge Montezuma cypress, or ahuehuete, that sits in the town square of Santa María del Tule in Oaxaca, Mexico.

www.discoverbajacalifornia.com

This is a tourist-focused website that includes maps, photographs, and video links showing Baja California.

www.latinamericanstudies.org/mexico-volcanoes.htm

This website provides information about volcanoes of Mexico along with photographs of and links to some of the most recent volcanic eruptions in Mexico.

www.visitmexico.com/wb/Visitmexico/ballena_gris

This web page provides broad coverage of gray-whale watching from Puerto Vallarta and Nayarit Riviera.

www.vivanatura.org/

This is a comprehensive site offering photos and video links of Mexico's rich and diverse animal and plant life.

HISTORY

El Castillo, often called the pyramid or the castle, at the Temple of Kukulcan is one of the most impressive monuments of the Mayan ruins of Chichén Itzá on the Yucatán Peninsula.

2

THE FIRST SETTLERS IN Mexico were nomadic hunter-gatherers who crossed the Bering Strait from Asia to Alaska in search of food. Traveling in small groups, they slowly moved south and eventually reached Mexico. Some groups went on as far south as Chile, but those who stayed behind began Mexico's earliest civilizations.

EARLY CIVILIZATIONS

The Olmec Indians developed the first highly civilized culture in Mesoamerica, around 1500 B.C. They passed on their culture to other groups through trade and war. Today the Olmec culture is thought to be the origin of many later Indian empires. The Olmec Indians were a tightly organized, very efficient group ruled by religious and civil leaders. They built religious centers on the gulf coast in southern Veracruz and Tabasco and established colonies in central and southern Mexico.

The most enduring legacy of the Olmec Indians is their art, especially their stone sculptures. Some of these sculptures feature heads with Asian and African features, suggesting that the Olmec population may have consisted of two ethnic groups. The remains of many of these monuments suggest the Olmec civilization came to a violent end around 400 B.C.

During the next 1,700 years, many cultures emerged. Some developed and flourished; others faded. Some of the more advanced were the Zapotecs and Mixtecs in southwestern Mexico and Monte Albán; the Tarascans of Michoacán; and the Totonacs of Veracruz, who built the famous Pyramid of the Niches in Tajín.

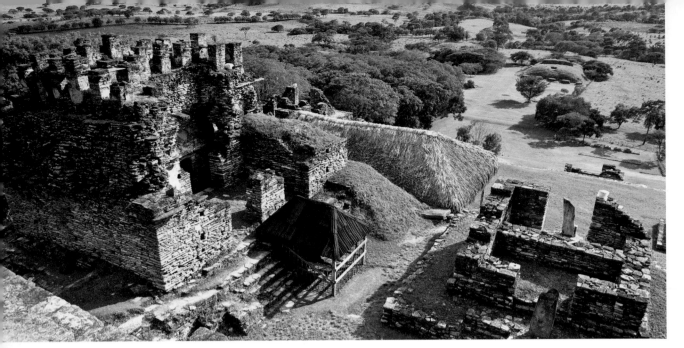

A view of the Toniná Mayan ruins in Chiapas. The Mayans were a highly artistic people who built beautiful cities. Many of their monuments have survived more than 1,000 years.

THE MAYANS

Perhaps the most spectacular culture in ancient Mexico, the Mayan civilization was the only one in the Americas to develop a system of writing used to record chronology, astronomy, history, and religion. Its system of mathematics was an achievement unequaled for centuries in Europe. The 365-day Mayan year was improved upon only in the 20th century. Mayan sculpture and architecture were unmatched in either beauty or dignity.

The Mayan civilization reached its peak between A.D. 250 and 800. The cities of Palenque and Tikal were the centers of a civilization that numbered more than 10 million people. The Mayan culture declined around A.D. 900. It is believed that the Mayans were hit by natural disasters and invaded by hostile groups. Today the remains of Mayan culture can be seen at impressive archaeological sites such as Chichén Itzá on the Yucatán Peninsula.

THE AZTECS

The Aztecs emerged faster and became more powerful than any other culture in the history of Mexico. Before their rise, they were a poor nomadic group living in the valleys of Mexico. By the time of the Spanish conquest in 1521, however, the Aztec Empire covered most of Mesoamerica.

In 1325 the Aztecs arrived on Lake Texcoco near present-day Mexico City. On an island in the middle of the lake, they spotted an eagle perched on a cactus holding a serpent in its mouth. The Aztecs interpreted this as a sign from the gods to settle there. They constructed a city called Tenochtitlán in that location. The eagle with the serpent in its mouth is the symbol of Mexico, and it appears on the country's flag and currency.

The first houses in Tenochtitlán were built on rafts in the middle of the shallow lake. After some 100 years, Tenochtitlán became an elegant, complex city. Meanwhile, the Aztecs became a sophisticated society of fierce warriors. Although Aztec society was dominated by the noble, priest, military, and merchant classes, it made provisions for the common people as well. For example, the education system was more advanced than in any other Mesoamerican civilization. Aztec culture had rich and complex mythological and religious traditions and was famed for its impressive architecture and artistic creations.

The Aztecs developed an aggressive, violent military culture dominated by a god of war. The army led many successful wars of conquest, and soldiers were rewarded with land grants and positions of wealth and influence.

As the Aztecs believed it was necessary to please their gods with human sacrifices, prisoners of war often met their end this way. Methods of sacrifice included drowning, whipping, and tearing hearts out of people while they were still alive.

An artist's impression of everyday life in the Aztec city of Tenochtitlán.

TEOTIHUACÁN

Teotihuacán is the largest, most impressive, and best known of all ancient Mexican religious centers. Built around 300 B.C. by Toltec Indians, it dominated the region until its mysterious decline and fall around A.D. 700. At its peak, Teotihuacán had a population of more than 200,000 and was Mexico's largest pre-Hispanic city.

Teotihuacán is laid out in a grid and dominated by the 215-feet-high (66-m-high) Pyramid of the Sun, the third-largest pyramid in the world. Other significant buildings in the city include the Pyramid of the Moon and the Temple of Quetzalcóatl.

The people of Teotihuacán were highly skilled artists. Their designs suggest their lives revolved around a complex religious system based on the worship of the sun god, the moon goddess, the rain god, and the god of civilization, Quetzalcóatl, whose name means "feathered serpent."

SPANISH CONQUEST

In 1519 Hernán Cortés (1485—1547) and about 500 Spanish adventurers known as conquistadores set sail in 11 ships for the New World of the Americas in search of treasure. Their arrival stunned the Aztecs, who had never seen ships, horses, or light-skinned people before.

An artist's impression of the meeting between Hernán Cortés and the Aztecs.

When word reached the Aztec emperor Moctezuma, the highly religious leader thought Cortés must be the God Quetzalcóatl, who legend said would return to Tenochtitlán that same year. To appease this "god" and get him to leave, Moctezuma sent gold, silver, and other riches to Cortés. When Cortés saw this treasure, he became determined to conquer the Aztecs and have all the wealth for himself.

Had Moctezuma fought Cortés's conquistadores immediately, it is unlikely the Spaniards would have survived, as they were vastly outnumbered by hundreds of thousands of Indians. Instead Cortés found a translator, La Malinche, a Náhuatl Indian woman who had been given to him as a slave girl by the Indians of Tabasco. La Malinche became his lover, adviser, and interpreter. Now that Cortés could communicate with the Indians, he kidnapped Moctezuma and formed alliances with the enemies of the Aztecs. A strategy of divide and conquer, combined with the Spaniards' sophisticated weaponry, was too much for the Aztecs. Though they fought bitterly and bravely, the Aztecs were soon conquered by Spain in 1521. From 1521 to 1524, Cortés was the governor of Mexico on behalf of the king of Spain, Charles V.

THE COLONIAL PERIOD

For 300 years under colonial rule, Mexico was governed by the Spanish crown, which issued decrees regulating every aspect of life. Mexico became the center of the vast Spanish empire known as New Spain, which included the Philippines and Guam across the Pacific, as well as Las Californias (present-day California, Nevada, Baja California, and Baja California Sur); Nueva

Extremadura (including present-day Texas); and Santa Fe de Nuevo México (including parts of New Mexico). New Spain's wealth was built on silver mining and trade between North America and Asia.

Spanish nobles ruled the vast lands taken from the decimated Aztecs with a system known as *encomienda* (en-koh-mee-YEN-dah), forcing the Indians to give tribute and labor to their Spanish landlords. The Spanish also established a social structure in Mexico. At the top of society were the *peninsulares* (pay-nin-soo-LAH-rehs), Spaniards born in Spain, who held political power. Next came the Creoles, who were Spaniards born in Mexico. Below them were the mestizos, who were of mixed Spanish and Indian blood. At the bottom of the social hierarchy were the Indians.

Another important event was the arrival of Catholic missionaries. Dedicated Catholic friars traveled through Mexico in their quest to convert the masses. Despite the Church's initial idealism, economic opportunities created practices that abused, neglected, and enslaved the Indians.

This painting depicts Padre Hidalgo, or Father Hidalgo, leading the local people and the church, united in the struggle against Spain.

The combination of imported diseases from Spain and abuses by the Spanish caused a huge number of Indian deaths. In one of the most catastrophic population declines in history, the Indian population fell from about 20 million in 1521 to just 2 million by 1580.

The composition of the population also changed significantly over this period. By 1810 there were an estimated 6 million inhabitants in New Spain, of whom 60,000 were Spanish-born, 940,000 were Creoles, 3.5 million were indigenous Mexicans, and 1.5 million were mestizos.

INDEPENDENCE

Although millions of Indians and mestizos suffered abuse because of inequalities in an extremely class-based society, it was the Creoles who led the movement for independence from Spain.

Resentful of Spain's interference in Mexico's burgeoning economy and inspired by ideas of individual rights and freedom from the American and French revolutions, the Creoles began pushing for change. On September 16, 1810, Father Miguel Hidalgo y Costilla (1753—1811), a 57-year-old parish priest from the town of Dolores, began the rebellion with the now-famous Grito de Dolores, or Cry of Dolores, demanding independence from Spain. The conflict lasted five years but failed. In 1820 the fight for independence was revived, with the Creoles and the *peninsulares* banding together. Their new army met with little resistance, and on September 27, 1821, the Treaty of Córdoba was signed, which recognized Mexican independence. A constitution was written and adopted in 1824. In the new constitution, the republic took the name of United Mexican States.

Having been weakened and divided by 300 years of Spanish domination, Mexico was not prepared for independence. Therefore, during the next 40 years, Mexico had 56 governments, including periodic rule by the dictator Antonio López de Santa Anna (1795—1876) over a 22-year-period. Santa Anna lost half of the country's territory to the United States, and he was finally overthrown in 1855 by an educated Indian named Benito Juárez (1806—72).

A photo of Benito Juárez.

BENITO JUÁREZ AND THE REFORM PERIOD

Benito Juárez, often called the Abraham Lincoln of Mexico, was a Zapotec Indian. He was orphaned as a young boy and raised by a Franciscan friar. Despite his strict Catholic upbringing, Juárez played an instrumental role in implementing reforms in the Catholic Church. Serving five terms as president of Mexico between 1858 and 1872, Juárez oversaw the transfer of political power from the Creoles to the mestizos.

The Catholic Church in 19th-century Mexico was far more wealthy and powerful than the Mexican government, yet it did little to bring about desperately needed political and social change. The Church was a conservative force that worked against any reforms that would weaken its power. Conflicts between church and state eventually led to a three-year civil war called the War of the Reform (1858—61) between the conservatives and liberal forces. Juárez led the liberals to victory and promptly instituted the reforms.

"Among individuals, as among nations, respect for the rights of others is peace."
–Benito Juárez, Mexican president (1861-72)

After the successful Texas Revolution of 1836, Texan settlers had established independent rule from Mexico. But a decade later Mexico and the United States fought each other in the Mexican-American War (1846—48). The war happened after the United States annexed the state of Texas, which Mexico claimed was part of its territory. Both countries claimed sovereignty over Texas, although the Texans wanted the state to become a part of the United States. The United States military was more powerful than Mexico's and was able to force a naval blockade of Mexican ports, as well as invade and conquer New Mexico, California, and parts of what is currently northern Mexico. An additional American army captured Mexico City, forcing Mexico to agree to the sale of its northern territories to the United States for $18 million.

Following the United States' victory, a treaty was drawn up (the Treaty of Guadalupe Hidalgo) that gave a vast tract of land to the Americans, including the present-day states of Arizona, Texas, New Mexico, Nevada, Utah, and California. Mexico was forced to accept the Rio Grande as its northern national border.

But in 1864 with the help of France, the Catholic Church regained power and exiled Juárez. France appointed an emperor of its choice, a well-intentioned Austrian prince named Maximilian. He tried to institute reforms to help the people, but because he was a foreigner, the people did not trust him.

After three years, with the help of the United States, Juárez was restored to power, and the reform laws became a permanent part of the Mexican government. When Juárez died in 1872, Mexico had a constitutional and democratic government.

THE PORFIRIATO

The death of Benito Juárez led to another period of instability, ultimately resulting in the dictatorship of Porfirio Díaz (1830—1915). Díaz was a mestizo who supported Juárez and his reform movement. But when he ran against Juárez for president in 1871 and lost, he claimed the election was fixed and that Juárez shouldn't be allowed to run for president so many times.

Yet once Díaz overthrew Juárez's successor, José María Iglesias, in 1876 and took over as head of the government, he ignored his own earlier protests and remained in power for 30 of the next 34 years. His ruthless dictatorship was so significant to Mexican history that this period is called the Porfiriato.

During the Porfiriato, the economy developed enormously, but social problems worsened. Many people who supported Díaz became rich, but the majority of the Mexican population lived in poverty. By 1910, 90 years after it gained independence, Mexico was a country with great social differences among the people. Most of the land and wealth were concentrated in the hands of about 20 percent of the population. The average peasant owned even less than he or she did before independence.

Díaz was a very shrewd man, but he caused his own downfall by telling a journalist that he was considering retirement. A relatively unknown Mexican named Francisco Madero (1873—1913) took Díaz at his word and ran against him for the presidency in 1910. At first Díaz did not take his opponent seriously, but Madero's campaign for political reform was so popular and so threatening to Díaz that finally the dictator had him imprisoned until after the election.

Pancho Villa (*left*) and Emiliano Zapata (*right*) fought against landed ranchers and the rich. Once seen as bandits, today they are revered as national heroes.

REVOLUTION AND REFORM

Francisco Madero strongly opposed violence, but he saw no other way to overthrow Díaz. So in November 1910 he called for rebellion. Bands of revolutionaries formed throughout Mexico.

In May 1911 Díaz was forced to resign. Madero was subsequently elected president through free and open elections. He formulated a program of economic reforms but was assassinated in a coup in 1913 before he could implement any changes.

After Madero's death, revolutionary leaders began to quarrel among themselves and with the new president, Venustiano Carranza (1859—1920). Two of these leaders, Emiliano Zapata (1879—1919) and Pancho Villa (1878—

1923), believed that reform through the political process was practically impossible. Instead they raised armies and forcibly took back land they believed rightfully belonged to the Indians and peasants. But Zapata and Villa were killed, and Carranza consolidated his power. Today Villa and Zapata are feted as national heroes.

In 1917 Carranza called a convention to prepare a new constitution. This constitution, still in effect today, laid the groundwork for a new Mexican nation. It limited presidents to one term; returned communal land to the peasants; gave the government control over education, the Catholic Church, and farm and oil properties; protected factory workers; and generally guaranteed basic democratic freedoms.

Decades of efforts at reform prevailed, and in 1934 the peaceful election of Lázaro Cárdenas (1895—1970) as the head of the Partido Revolucionario Institucional (Institutional Revolutionary Party), referred to as the PRI, symbolized the success of the revolution. Cárdenas distributed land, made loans available to peasants, organized workers' and peasants' confederations, and expropriated and nationalized foreign-owned industries, in particular the petroleum industry. His presidency saw six years of impressive economic growth and the fulfillment of many of the revolution's ideals, as well as provided the stable basis for contemporary Mexico.

MODERN TIMES

Although the ruling PRI initiated solid economic growth for almost 40 years, the government's policies led to social unrest in the 1960s, culminating in the massacre of protesters at Tlatelolco in 1968. Economic crises also swept the country in 1976 and 1982, leading to the devaluation of the Mexican currency, the peso. Environmental disasters had an impact as well: On September 19, 1985, a huge earthquake struck Michoacán, inflicting severe damage on Mexico City and killing an estimated 10,000 people.

Another economic crisis in 1995 weakened the government of President Ernesto Zedillo, who was challenged by the appearance of the Zapatista Army of National Liberation (Ejército Zapatista de Liberación Nacional, EZLN), a revolutionary leftist group based in Chiapas, the southernmost state of Mexico. Uprisings in the Chiapas region led by the Zapatistas resulted in the deaths of at least 100 people in 1993 and 1994. Responding to public demands, Zedillo oversaw political and electoral reforms that reduced the PRI's hold on power. On July 2, 2000, Vicente Fox Quesada, the candidate of the National Action Party (Partido Acción Nacional, PAN), was elected the 69th president of Mexico, ending the PRI's 71-year-long control of the office. He was elected on a platform that promoted the modernization of labor laws and encouraged private investment in the energy sector and the country's infrastructure. On September 5, 2006, PAN candidate Felipe Calderón Hinojosa won the presidency, after one of the most hotly contested elections in recent Mexican history.

INTERNET LINKS

www.whc.unesco.org/en

This World Heritage Convention website provides comprehensive information, including photographs and maps, about the holy city of Teotihuacán.

www.mexconnect.com/tags/historical-sites

This is Mexico's premier English-language online magazine site, which offers links to articles and photographs on many of Mexico's major historical sites, as well as on some lesser-known places, such as the Dos Estrellas haunted mine.

www.aztec-history.net/

This website offers detailed descriptions, pictures, and links on every aspect of Aztec culture and civilization.

http://users.erols.com/mwhite28/mexico.htm

This website on the Mexican Revolution presents a series of colorful maps illustrating development of the revolution in five stages.

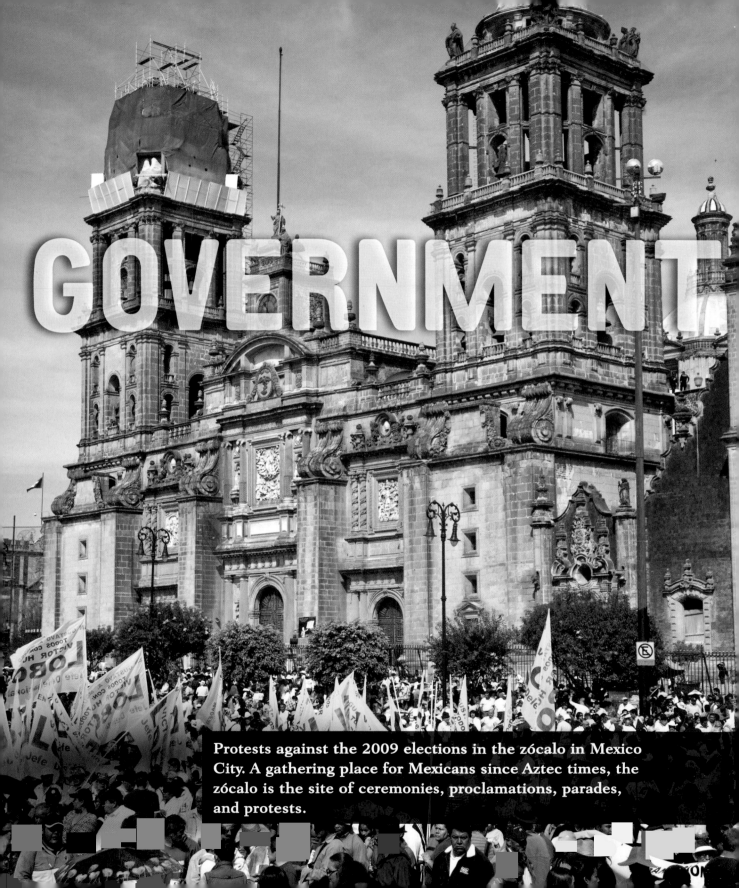

GOVERNMENT

Protests against the 2009 elections in the zócalo in Mexico City. A gathering place for Mexicans since Aztec times, the zócalo is the site of ceremonies, proclamations, parades, and protests.

3

MEXICO IS A FEDERAL REPUBLIC divided into 31 states and a federal district containing the capital, Mexico City. The official name of the country is Estados Unidos Mexicanos, or the United Mexican States.

THE 1917 CONSTITUTION

The government is based on the constitution of 1917, which attempts to fulfill the goals fought for during the Mexican Revolution and the following period and to create a structure that both eliminates past abuses and prevents future ones.

The Palacio Nacional, or National Palace, faces the east side of the *zócalo*, one of the world's largest open squares.

The constitution divides the government into three branches: executive, legislative, and judicial. It also establishes state governments with elected governors and legislatures.

Under the constitution, the federal government has great power in economic, educational, and state matters. The government used this power for the benefit of the people when it divided privately owned farmlands among the poor and when it set up a national school system. Other uses of this power have been more controversial, such as when the government nationalized the railroad and oil industries, taking them over. The federal government also has the authority to suspend a state's constitutional powers and has done so in the past to settle state power struggles. Although the Mexican government still struggles with a weak economy and political corruption, it has become more stable since the establishment of the constitution of 1917.

NATIONAL GOVERNMENT

The Supreme Court near Mexico City's *zócalo.*

The executive branch of the Mexican government is headed by a president who is elected for a six-year term. There is no vice president. If a president does not finish his term, the congress chooses a temporary president to serve until a special or a regular election is held. The president cannot run for reelection.

The legislative branch is called the congress. It is divided into two branches: the senate and the chamber of deputies. The senate has 128 senators, each elected to serve a six-year term. The chamber of deputies has 500 members, each elected for a three-year term. Members of congress cannot serve two consecutive terms.

The judicial system is headed by the Supreme Court of Justice, made up of 21 regular members and five presidential appointees. There are also 32 state-level courts serving the 31 states and the federal district.

STATE AND LOCAL GOVERNMENTS

Mexico's states are each headed by a governor. State governors are elected to six-year terms and cannot run for reelection. The chamber of deputies in each state has 9 to 25 members. They too are not allowed to serve more than one term in office. The president appoints the chief of the federal district, where the presidential residence, congress, and the Supreme Court are located.

Each state is divided into cities or townships called *municipios* (moo-nee-SEE-pee-ohs). There are about 2,400 *municipios* in Mexico, each headed by a municipal president and a town council. All officers of the local government are elected by the citizens.

THE ARMY

Unlike the armed forces in most other Latin American countries, the Mexican army plays a very insignificant role in governing the republic. Realizing the importance of having the army under their control, Mexican presidents have richly rewarded army loyalty and severely punished acts of betrayal.

As Mexico is unlikely to enter into war with any of its neighbors, Mexican presidents have consistently reduced the army's share of the federal budget. Mexico has one of the lowest ratios of soldiers to population in Latin America. Since 1920 Mexico has been the only Latin American country whose government has not experienced an attempted coup.

Military service is mandatory at age 18 for all males for a period of 12 months. Conscripts are allowed to serve only in the army; all naval and air force personnel have to be volunteers.

POLITICAL PARTIES

Until the 21st century, the strongest political party in Mexico was the PRI. It was created in 1929 to serve as the official party for the economic and social

One of the contributing factors to Mexico's political stability is the army's nonpolitical role.

U.S.-MEXICAN RELATIONS

Most U.S. citizens don't realize how much the fate of their country is bound with that of Mexico. Due to geographical proximity, what happens in Mexico greatly affects the United States. The two countries share a 1,969-mile-long (3,169-km-long) border, much of which is unguarded. While there appears to be no great threat as yet, should unrest in Mexico force the United States to establish border defenses, the cost would be enormous.

Mexico's need to import goods from the United States has created hundreds of thousands of jobs in the United States. Mexico is the United States' third largest trading partner (after Canada and China), whereas the United States is Mexico's largest market: Mexico sells 80 percent of its goods and services north of the border.

Mexican-Americans are an important political force in the United States. U.S. citizens are increasingly exposed to Mexican culture and sensitivities, particularly in cities with large Mexican-American populations.

However, there are tensions in the relationship. A very large proportion of the illegal drugs brought into the United States are controlled by drug cartels (syndicates) in Mexico. Mexico has become a major producer of heroin and marijuana for illegal export to the United States. Also, as much as 90 percent of the cocaine that arrives in the United States from South America transits through Mexico. Both the U.S. and Mexican governments have spent billions of dollars fighting the illegal drug trade but to limited effect—the drug cartels make too much money from it, and the demand for illegal drugs remains strong.

The Mexican border is also the biggest source of illegal immigration into the United States each year. U.S. government figures show that more than 50 percent of illegal immigrants are Mexicans. Most of these immigrants go to the United States to earn more money and make a better life for themselves. Most work in construction, farming, manufacturing, and service-based industries in the states that border Mexico, especially California and Texas. Many Mexicans who work in the United States send money home to their families. In 2003 the then-president of Mexico, Vicente Fox, stated that remittances "are our biggest source of foreign income, bigger than oil, tourism, or foreign investment." In 2005 the World Bank estimated that Mexico was receiving $18.1 billion in remittances every year.

goals of the Mexican Revolution. It represents almost every major power group in the nation, including labor unions, the business community, financial interests, and peasant movements.

Until 2000 the PRI had won every presidential election by a huge majority. In recent years, however, other parties, such as the PAN and the Partido de la Revolución Democrática (Party of Democratic Revolution), or PRD, have played a much larger role in national politics. The current president is Felipe de Jesus Calderón from the PAN, who was elected in December 2006 with 35.9 percent of the votes, just a fraction ahead of his nearest rival, Andrés Manuel López Obrador. In the national elections in 2006 the PAN had the largest number of votes, gaining 206 seats in the chamber of deputies, followed by the PRD with 127 seats, and the PRI with 106 seats. In the senate, the PAN again dominated, gaining 52 seats, compared with the PRI, with 35 seats. Despite falling behind on the national level, more states are governed by the PRI than by any other party. An era of multiparty politics has begun in Mexico.

Felipe Calderón during a ceremony.

INTERNET LINKS

www.mexperience.com/living/mexico-society-culture.php#3

This website provides a brief outline of Mexican politics, a description of the main parties, plus coverage of both the police force and the military and their roles in modern Mexican politics.

http://geo-mexico.com/?p=1786

This website gives concise coverage of the 2010 national elections, with a colorful map that makes understanding the results easier.

www.bbc.co.uk/news/world-latin-america-12242685

The BBC News website offers a brief profile of Mexico's current president, Felipe Calderón, with analysis, photographs, and links.

ECONOMY

The dome-shaped Mexican Stock Exchange is accompanied by other skyscapers in the financial district of Paseo de La Reforma in Mexico City.

4

THE MODERN MEXICAN ECONOMY is based on manufacturing, industry, and international trade. While agriculture is still important, trade and manufacturing make up the major economic sectors. The Mexican economy is the 13th-largest in the world, making Mexico an important economic player.

In the 1970s vast oil reserves were discovered along Mexico's eastern coast. Income from oil production fueled industrial development. While the price of oil was high, Mexico borrowed money for construction projects and to finance economic and social development programs. It planned to pay back the debt through oil sales.

The port docks of Veracruz, a major port city on the Gulf of Mexico.

Oil prices fell in the early 1980s, however, and Mexico found itself in debt without enough money to pay back the loans. In 2000 the national debt stood at approximately $150 billion, and by 2010 the debt had risen to $212 billion. This debt remains a serious problem for the Mexican government. Mexico has attempted, with some success, to trade its way out of debt. The Mexican economy grew at an average rate of 5.1 percent during 1995—2002.

Typical earnings in Mexico in 2010 were $13,800 per year. The majority of Mexicans (62.9 percent) were employed in the service sector, while 23.4 percent worked in industry, and a much smaller 4.2 percent were employed in the historically important agricultural sector. Massive differences in wealth remain, with a huge gap between the rich and the poor. One of the government's most important tasks is to reduce income inequality, especially between urban and rural Mexicans.

Despite the enactment of NAFTA and financial aid from the United States, Mexico suffered a serious financial crisis in 1994, from which it took years to recover. In the recent world economic recession of 2008—09, the Mexican economy did shrink (by 6.5 percent in 2009), but the downturn had much less effect on people's everyday lives, as unemployment rose only a little and wages remained stable. The economy grew by 5 percent in 2010, with exports, especially to the United States, leading the way.

Autonomous in exercising its functions, the Banco de Mexico, or the National Bank of Mexico, aims to maintain the stability of the people's purchasing power by controlling the currency.

NAFTA

Certain sectors of Mexico's economy grew with the implementation of NAFTA in 1994. NAFTA established a trading area that consists of Canada, the United States, and Mexico, with significantly reduced trade tariffs and greater economic cooperation. Since the implementation of NAFTA, Mexico's share of U.S. exports has increased from 7 percent to 12 percent, and its share of Canadian exports has doubled to 5 percent.

Although the United States is already Mexico's most important trade partner, accounting for well over half of Mexico's exports and imports, NAFTA has encouraged an even stronger trade relationship between the two countries. Unfortunately the benefits of this trade have not been evenly distributed around the country, and some poor Mexicans have tried to resist open-trade policies.

Mexico also has free-trade agreements with more than 40 other countries worldwide, helping the country's economy to prosper.

A beer bottling plant in Monterrey. With available skilled labor, Mexico is industrializing at a rapid pace.

SOURCES OF REVENUE

Mexicans often talk about the extreme generosity God showed them when creating the country's natural resources: oil; timber; large deposits of gold, silver, and other valuable metals; rivers providing natural irrigation and hydroelectric power; beautiful coastlines (5,797 miles/9,330 km); waters filled with fish; and mountains full of game. These natural resources are the foundation of Mexico's economy, with great income-generating potential in mining, agriculture, manufacturing, and tourism.

MANUFACTURING Mexico's transformation from a primarily agricultural economy to an industrial one is largely due to its relatively new oil industry.

Almost half of the country's manufacturing activity takes place in Mexico City and its suburbs. This area is Mexico's leading industrial center, which consists of factories manufacturing automobiles, consumer products, pharmaceutical products, and textiles. The financial, construction, hotel

An offshore drilling platform in the harbor of Galveston. Mexico's economy can be described as industrial rather than agricultural.

and restaurant, and retail sectors are also concentrated in Mexico City. Guadalajara and Monterrey are other important industrial cities. The Monterrey Institute of Technology trains some of the country's best engineers.

Mexico's most important products include farm machinery, chemicals, clothing, iron and steel, processed foods, petroleum, beer, rubber, wood pulp, and paper. International carmakers such as General Motors, Ford, Volkswagen, and Chrysler manufacture cars and auto parts in Mexico. The National Railroad Car factory supplies most of the cars and equipment used by Mexico's railway system.

The fast growth of manufacturing in Mexico since the 1940s has affected the entire economy. The production of raw materials for new factories has increased, and banking, marketing, and other service industries have expanded. Heavy government spending on construction has provided additional housing for the growing industrial centers. Power plants have been built to generate electricity for the new industries. New highways and railroads have been constructed to carry both raw materials and finished goods to make communications more efficient.

ELECTRONICS The electronics industry in Mexico has grown enormously since 2000. In 2007 Mexico became the world's largest manufacturer of televisions, and in 2008 it surpassed China, South Korea, and Taiwan to become the largest producer of smartphones in the world. In 2008 one out of every four consumer appliances sold in the United States came from Mexico. In 2009 Mexico's fastest-growing corporation was Lanix, a manufacturer and designer of computers, servers, and other high-tech electronic products.

AGRICULTURE Ever since the early Indians cultivated wild corn on *ejidos* (eh-HEE-dohs), or communal plots, Mexico was a predominantly agricultural country. For most of Mexico's history, the majority of its people lived off the land. After the Spanish conquest, most of the land in Mexico was organized into huge estates called haciendas that were owned by wealthy landlords. After the revolution of 1910 the new government divided most of them back into *ejidos* and distributed them to landless peasants. In 1970 agriculture made up 25 percent of Mexico's economy. Today, however, farming plays only a small role in the economy of the country, contributing less than 4 percent.

Although only about one-third of Mexican land can be farmed, many Mexicans manage to survive by growing crops anywhere they can. It is not unusual, for instance, to see corn growing on a rocky slope.

The kinds of crops grown in Mexico vary, depending on the altitude, rainfall, and temperature of the different regions. The southern part of Mexico's Central Plateau contains the best farmland. The dry northern part of the plateau is used mainly for cattle grazing, although irrigation projects have developed some cropland.

The wet, hot regions of southern and eastern Mexico and the eastern coastal plains require much work to turn them into productive farmlands. This work includes clearing and draining the land and controlling floods, insects, and plant diseases.

Mexico is self-sufficient in cotton, which is cultivated mainly in the northwestern part of the country. Sisal fiber, obtained from henequen leaves and used for making rope and rugs, is a major product of the Yucatán area.

MINING It was Mexico's vast amounts of gold and silver that attracted Cortés and the Spanish conquistadores to its shores. Today the country still has large deposits of gold and silver as well as copper, lead, zinc, petroleum, iron ore, and sulfur.

An aerial view of farm plots in the Toluca Valley, southwest of Mexico City. Mexico's harsh terrain makes it extremely difficult to grow enough food for the entire population. Most of the country is unsuitable for agriculture, as it either is mountainous or receives little rainfall.

TOURISM

The tourist industry is extremely vital to Mexico's economy. It is often called the "industry without chimneys." Indeed, the Mexican government promotes tourism as an economic asset. Mexico is the number-one destination for foreign tourists in Latin America and the second most popular destination in the Americas. Close to 20 million tourists visit Mexico each year, making Mexico the eighth most visited country in the world. Winter is the busy season for tourism, as the weather is cooler around this time. Typical tourist destinations are Mexico City and the ruins of ancient Mayan and Aztec cities. The most popular beach resorts include Acapulco, Ensenada, Manzanillo, Mazatlán, Puerto Vallarta, Cancún, and Cozumel Island. In the past decade, about 85 percent of visitors to Mexico were from the United States. In addition, about 60 million brief crossings are made each year by Americans for shopping, dining, or auto-repair purposes, rather than for actual vacations.

The Central Plateau is the country's most heavily mineralized region. Each year Mexico mines about one-sixth of the world's total production of silver, making it the world's leading producer of silver.

Mexico has some of the largest oil reserves in the Western Hemisphere, approximately the size of the oil reserves in Saudi Arabia. As a result, Mexico has become one of the world's leading producers of petroleum, pumping about 3.7 million barrels per day. All mineral resources are considered national property by law, and the petroleum industry is operated by the government. However, oil is not as important today as in previous decades—in 1980 oil accounted for 61 percent of total exports; by 2000 it was only 7.3 percent.

OTHER SERVICES Employing almost two-thirds of the working population, the service sector includes transportation, commerce, warehousing, restaurants and hotels, arts and entertainment, health, education, financial and banking services, and telecommunications, as well as defense and public administration.

INTERNET LINKS

www.cancunsouth.com/act_ecotour.html

This website is a guide to ecotourism in the Mexican state of Cancún, with descriptions, advice, photographs, and links.

www.sciencedaily.com/releases/2007/04/070409181647.htm

The articles on this website explore some of the earliest evidence of corn and its farming in Mexico, some of which date from more than 7,000 years ago.

www.naftaworks.org/

This website provides an easy understanding and serves as a guide to NAFTA, including explanations of how the institution works, its core benefits, and its members.

ENVIRONMENT

Rock formations spring from the middle of the ocean in Cabo San Lucas on the gulf of Baja California.

5

MEXICO IS HOME TO AN incredibly wide variety of plants and animals. The country is ranked first in the world for its variety of reptiles, with 707 known species; second for mammals, with 438 species; fourth for amphibians, with 290 species; and fourth for flora, with 26,000 species.

As a developing country trying to improve its economy and provide for its citizens, however, Mexico faces many challenges when it comes to protecting its natural treasures for future generations.

MEXICO'S TREASURES

Forming a bridge between the rest of North America and the isthmus of Central America, Mexico has unique geographical characteristics. Spanning both temperate and tropical zones, the country is located at a latitude where most of the world's deserts have developed. Different climates and ecosystems occurring at varying altitudes in the mountainous regions have created an incredible degree of biodiversity.

The dry semideserts in the north are home to coyotes, pumas, armadillos, and deer, whereas the southern tropical forests support jaguars, ocelots, tapirs, and anteaters. Numerous types of vegetation are found, including deciduous and coniferous forests. Mexico has 35 species of pine, as well as coastal mangrove forests and semiarid plains.

Mexico's coastal waters harbor whales, seals, dolphins, and sea lions, and the beaches are breeding grounds for sea turtles. Most species of sea turtle are endangered due to overhunting and loss of habitat. The turtles are hunted for their skins, which can be used to make boots. Bird life is equally diverse—eagles and ospreys live in the north, while parrots, macaws, and toucans are common in the south. Reptiles abound in the tropical forests, the most spectacular being the boa constrictor. Blessed with remarkable diversity, Mexico is a cornucopia of life.

HUMAN IMPACT

The impact of human activity on the environment has been severe. About two-thirds of the country was forested at the time of the Spanish conquest; only one-fifth remains forested today, and this area is shrinking. Scientists estimate that between 1990 and 2010 Mexico lost an average of 678,181 acres (274,450 ha), or 0.39 percent, of its forest cover per year. In total, between 1990 and 2010, Mexico lost 7.8 percent of its forests, or around 13,563,614 acres (5,489,000 ha).

Some of the pressure on forest ecosystems comes from the logging industry in Mexico; another major contributor is human settlement. Illegal logging and poaching are widespread in Mexico. Criminal gangs dominate the illegal timber trade, and national parks, although protected, are common targets for wood extraction. As people move into new areas, they clear the land for agriculture using the traditional slash-and-burn method. In dry years fires that are started to clear land can spread into virgin forests. In 1998 widespread fires destroyed nearly 1.5 million acres (600,000 ha) of forest and scrubland and sent thick smoke into the air as far north as Canada. Several southern U.S. states issued health warnings, and the United States sent firefighters and helicopters to help battle the blazes. Such fires result in the loss of plant and animal habitats and can eventually cause the extinction of species. In the dry north, overgrazing by cattle and excessive irrigation to extend farmlands has led to soil degradation and erosion.

The coasts are also in danger. Spills from oil tankers in the Gulf of Mexico have destroyed marine habitats. Tourism, a growing industry, has brought thousands of people to the beaches, leaving huge amounts of waste to pollute the sand and water. Without proper facilities, waste often gets dumped in the ocean.

CRITICALLY ENDANGERED SPECIES

Because of Mexico's huge biological diversity, the Mexican government has laws to protect more than 2,000 species. In Mexico today the following animals are listed as critically endangered, meaning they are in danger of becoming extinct, by the International Union for Conservation of Nature (IUCN):

- *Chiapan climbing rat*
- *Margarita Island kangaroo rat*
- *Oaxacan pocket gopher*
- *Omiltemi rabbit*
- *Querétaro pocket gopher*
- *Slevin's mouse*
- *Tumbala climbing rat*

An additional 30 species are considered endangered, and at least 30 are categorized as vulnerable.

THE MAQUILADORA BORDERLANDS

Pollution is one of Mexico's most critical environmental problems. Places such as Tijuana are dangerously polluted with heavy metals, solvents, and acids from *maquilas* (mah-KEE-lahs) located along the border between Mexico and the United States. *Maquilas* are factories owned by foreigners. The Mexican government allows *maquilas* to import parts for Mexican workers to assemble and then to export assembled products. The first *maquila* began in 1965 as part of a program to create jobs in Mexico. The big *maquila* owners are U.S. companies, which find the maquiladora borderlands a convenient location for transportation of goods to U.S. markets. In the first decade of the 21st century, *maquila* companies accounted for half of all Mexican exports to the United States, making this type of factory an important part of the Mexican economy.

Children and their parents work all day sifting trash for items to sell and scraps to eat at the Santa Fe refuse dump near Mexico City.

Until 2001 *maquilas* were required to export any waste they produced. Under NAFTA, however, that rule was dropped. Areas around the maquiladora borderlands have become industrial dumping grounds, and exposure to industrial pollutants poses a health risk to *maquila* workers.

THE FEDERAL DISTRICT: AN UNHEALTHY PLACE

Home to roughly 20 million people, Mexico City is one of the largest metropolitan areas in the world. Mexico City's air quality has gone from among the world's cleanest to among the dirtiest in the span of a generation. In the 1950s residents of Mexico City could see for tens of miles beyond the city limits; today the average visibility is just a few miles at best, the view blocked by the choking smog. Mexico City is nestled in a valley and surrounded on three sides by mountains. This provides perfect conditions for smog to get trapped in the capital. Ground-level ozone and dust exceed national standards for 80 percent of the year, affecting the health and quality of life of all its residents. In addition, Mexicans from rural areas swarm to Mexico City—the country's economic hub—looking for work. They crowd the city and suburbs, increasing the amount of waste.

The main cause of pollution in Mexico City is emissions from cars, trucks, and buses, especially heavy vehicles using diesel fuel. The 3 million vehicles in the city contribute some 80 percent of the 5 million tons (4.54 billion kg) of contaminants released into the city's atmosphere annually. When the No Driving Day program was implemented to ban driving on certain days according to license plate number, wealthy car owners went out and bought themselves another car, thus worsening the city's pollution problem. Pollution in Mexico City also filters into surrounding areas. Biological waste produced by the city's millions of residents contaminates river systems flowing out of the valley. While Mexico City's problems are not unique, they pose a great challenge to the country's environmental agencies and economic planners.

SOLUTIONS

Mexicans are aware of the natural treasures they possess and make efforts to protect them. The government has designated a number of protected areas around the country in an effort to preserve the country's flora and fauna. But Mexico cannot solve its pollution problem without outside help. Pressure to manufacture goods for export forces Mexican industries to produce cheaply in order to meet demand and beat competition. Cheap production methods and outdated technology pollute the environment.

As a NAFTA member, Mexico needs the support of the United States and Canada to gain access to safer technologies and resist the pressure to produce goods cheaply at the cost of the environment.

THE REAL TREASURES OF THE SIERRA MADRE

One ray of hope for Mexico's environment is the commitment of the indigenous peoples to protect their land. This is illustrated in the efforts of the Huichols. The Huichols are Amerindians who have succeeded in preserving most of their culture and environment due to their isolation in the traditionally impenetrable Sierra Madre. However, outsiders found their way to the mountains and began destroying the environment. As water was drained away to support the thriving city of Guadalajara, the forests of the Sierra Madre began to disappear, as did animals living in the region, such as the white-tailed deer.

Once a thriving habitat, this mangrove forest on the gulf coast of Celestún in Yucatán has been wiped out by pollution.

"The Huichols teach us that man must be a steward of the Earth, he must feel in his heart the pain of the wounded animal, the crushed blade of grass. For all souls are linked." –Charmayne McGee, author of *So Sings the Blue Deer* (1997)

EL VIZCAÍNO: NURSERY FOR GRAY WHALES

El Vizcaíno Biosphere Reserve is near the center of Baja California, in the state of Baja California Sur. With a landmass of more than 55,444 square miles (143,600 square km) it is the largest and most diverse wildlife refuge in Latin America. This area was declared a protected zone in 1971, and in 1993 it became a UNESCO World Heritage Site. Each year the lagoons located in this area serve as nurseries or kindergartens for female gray whales and their newborn calves. The gray whale lives along the coast of North America, traveling from the Bering Sea off Alaska, where it spends the summers, to Baja California for winter feeding and birthing. This amazing journey of 5,600 miles (9,012 km) is one of the longest known migrations in the animal world.

Grays are whalebone whales, meaning that they have long strips of fibrous baleen, an elastic substance, in their mouths to sift out food. Gray whales are unique because, unlike other baleen whales that sift through ocean water, they feed at the bottom of the ocean, straining silt and mud through the baleen as they look for invertebrates to eat. A female gray whale reaches 46 feet (14 m) in length and can weigh 70,000 pounds (31,751 kg), whereas the male is shorter at 43 feet (13 m). The calves are born at an amazing length of 16 feet (5 m)!

There are about 26,000 gray whales in existence today. But in 1946 they were on the brink of extinction due to whale hunting. El Vizcaíno has played an important role in saving the gray whale from certain death. In recent years the IUCN classified the gray whale as being of "least concern" from a conservation perspective, downgrading its protected status. However, the specific subpopulation in the northwest Pacific is regarded as being "critically endangered." The northwest Pacific population is also listed as endangered by the U.S. Government National Marine Fisheries Service under the U.S. Endangered Species Act.

The Huichols, seeing themselves as stewards of the planet, decided to take action. In 1986 they made a 600-mile (966-km) pilgrimage to Mexico City to ask the government for a white-tailed deer from one of the city's zoos; they were given 20 to revive the white-tailed deer population in the Sierra Madre. Huichol elders now work with the National Indigenous Institute on educational, economic, and health programs. The Huichols were awarded Mexico's National Ecology Prize in 1988 for their efforts to save the environment. More recently, in 2009, the Huichols were involved in a dispute with a Canadian mining company over the company's purchase of mineral rights in the area of Wirikuta Mountain, one of the tribe's most sacred locations. The mining company practices open-case mining, which ruins the local environment and destroys habitats.

NATIONAL PARKS

In Mexico there are 93 protected areas that cover 45,173 square miles (11.7 million ha), roughly 6 percent of the nation. These protected areas have different statuses and include biosphere reserves, national parks, national marine parks, and natural monuments. Most of the national parks were created in the 1930s, when 40 were designated, based on criteria such as scenic beauty, recreational potential, and ecological value. National parks are home to many of Mexico's volcanoes, as well as to many of the country's archaeological sites.

A white-tailed deer at a park in Mexico. Although they were once widespread in the forests, their numbers have been considerably reduced due to industrialization.

Mexico's many national parks include the Cañón del Sumidero in Chiapas, which is home to a rich ecosystem and one of the most impressive canyons in the world. The Sumidero Canyon is 3,281 feet (1,000 m) deep, and its cliffs overlook the Grijalva River, which is home to the American crocodile, one of the park's largest and fiercest residents.

The Palenque National Park (4,389 acres/1,776 ha) is home to one of Mexico's most important archaeological sites, the Palenque Mayan ruins, which date back to 800 B.C. Although smaller than the sites at Copán and Tikal, Palenque contains some of the finest stone carvings, roof combs, and sculptures of the Mayan civilization.

PIRATES OR PROSPECTORS?

An important reason for preserving the natural environment is that it may hold many undiscovered cures for illnesses. This is particularly true of plants in tropical rain forests, which have not yet been fully explored by scientists. Indigenous groups that have lived in these regions for thousands of years know a great deal about tropical wildlife. The Mayans of the state of Chiapas are one such group.

Western scientists and pharmaceutical companies have realized that indigenous knowledge of the natural environment may hold the key to curing diseases such as arthritis and AIDS. The issue at stake is the rights to ownership of this information. Some argue that indigenous people own their knowledge, whereas others say that pharmaceutical companies have the right to gain profit from the drugs they make based on indigenous knowledge; still others argue that this information should be shared freely for the benefit of all humanity.

There is an ongoing conflict between the Mayans and industrial groups eager to explore or "prospect" for new drugs in Chiapas. Mayan folk healers fear that scientists will claim ownership over what really belongs to the Mayas. The United Nations' Treaty on Biodiversity states that indigenous interests must be protected, but many nations, including the United States, have not signed this treaty. There may be no easy answer to the question of ownership of new knowledge, but it is clear that it is in everyone's interest to protect and preserve the environment.

Biosphere reserves are areas of ecological diversity. The reserves all have an area greater than 24,711 acres (10,000 ha). These parks are inhabited by species that are considered to be threatened or in danger of extinction. All Mexican biosphere reserves are closely managed by the government and are committed to sustainable conservation. People often live in these reserves but in ways that are compatible with the preservation of the environment. In the biosphere reserves, Mexico has pioneered the use of a zoning system that allows some parts to be used for tourism and other economic activities, whereas other areas are out of bounds except for scientific study.

Located in the center of the Baja California Peninsula, El Vizcaíno Biosphere Reserve is the largest wildlife refuge in Latin America. Despite its extreme desert climate and strong winds, El Vizcaíno is home to an incredible diversity of wildlife. Coyotes, rodents, and hares all survive in these conditions, as does the California pronghorn, one of the fastest animals on earth. Desert bighorn sheep also live here, as do migratory birds—such as ospreys, cormorants, and herons—and marine life, such as dolphins, gray whales, and California sea lions.

The Sian Ka'an Biosphere Reserve in the Yucatán Peninsula is remarkable for its tropical rain forest, saltwater marshes, and mangroves, as well as for being home to a stretch of the Mesoamerican Barrier Reef. Created by presidential decree in 1986 and made a World Heritage site in 1987, this sparsely populated area sprawls for 1.3 million acres (540,000 ha) along the coast near Tulum. All five species of Mexican wildcat—jaguar, puma, ocelot, margay, and jaguarondi—live here. The reserve is also home to more than 300 species of birds, marine turtles, and the extremely rare West Indian manatee.

INTERNET LINKS

http://cesiak.org/

The website for the Centro Ecologico Sian Ka'an (CESiaK) Biosphere Reserve in Mexico includes links and photographs.

http://rainforests.mongabay.com/20mexico.htm

This website offers broad coverage of all the environmental issues affecting Mexico in the 21st century, with numerous statistics, links, and photographs.

www.whaleroute.com/areas/mexico/index.htm

This website provides descriptions and images of gray whales and discusses their movement around the Pacific coast of Mexico.

www.sciencedaily.com/releases/2010/04/100428153256.htm

This web page offers a scientific view of the effects of air pollution on young people in Mexico City.

MEXICANS

An Indian woman in her traditional Tehuantepec costume in Oaxaca.

6

A CENSUS CONDUCTED IN 2010 showed that Mexico had a population of 112,322,757 people, making it the most populous Spanish-speaking country in the world. In 1900 the population was just 13 million—so the country has expanded almost tenfold over the past 110 years.

Olmec head sculpture with African features. Whether people with these features actually lived in Mexico is a mystery. It is believed that the Olmecs had no contact with any foreign civilizations, as their languages were unlike those in other parts of the world, and no relics from other civilizations have been found.

SOCIAL HIERARCHY

Mexico is an extremely class-conscious society. The Spanish conquest was followed by centuries of oppression of the indigenous population. After achieving independence, the new ruling class of Creoles and mestizos continued to discriminate against Indians. Not until after the revolution of 1910 were efforts made to advance the position of the Indians socially and economically. But while the government tries to promote Indian accomplishments and culture, Mexican society still treats pure-blooded Indians as social inferiors.

Many Indians have a deep-seated sense of inferiority stemming from various historical and social factors. For example, the Mexican ideal of beauty, as perpetuated in the media, encompasses light skin, blue eyes, and blond hair—typically European features. Also, high rates of poverty and illiteracy among Mexican Indians make them the most vulnerable group during economic recession. In addition, the practice of human sacrifice and cannibalism among some Indian groups before the Spanish conquest can be a source of shame to present-day Indians.

A local getting his shoes polished by an Indian.

INDIANS

Mexican Indians are descendants of a pre-Hispanic people who migrated from Asia to America. Evidence of Mexico's Asian roots exists even today. Many Mexicans still have Asian features, and in some very fundamental ways native Mexican culture and people are more Asian than Western.

Mexico has approximately 10 million Indians, divided into 62 recognized ethnic and language groups, with more than 100 dialects. Most of these groups live in the Central Plateau, in the southern Pacific coastal states of Oaxaca, Chiapas, and Guerrero, and in Yucatán and Veracruz on the gulf coast. According to official statistics, only a little more than half of them

THE HUICHOLS: A WINDOW TO THE PAST

A group of around 15,000 Huichol Indians live in the Sierra Madre. In the past, this remote location and rugged mountainous terrain protected the Huichols from the abuse of the conquistadores and the influence of the Catholic missionaries.

Having preserved their pre-Columbian traditions, the Huichols offer a fascinating window to Mexico's pre-Spanish past. Huichol shamans practice healing rituals as they have for generations. Perhaps their survival is partly the result of their focus on tradition. The Huichols are most popularly known for their ritual use of peyote, a type of cactus that has hallucinogenic effects. Peyote is used for planting, harvesting, and deer-hunting ceremonies. The soil and climate of the Huichols' land are not ideal for growing peyote, however, so the Huichols make an annual pilgrimage to the desert of San Luis Potosí to find the cactus.

So far there has been no serious threat to the Huichol way of life, either from mestizos or from the rapid expansion of tourism in recent years. The Mexican government has also been sympathetic to the Huichols' desire to preserve their ancient culture.

(5.4 percent of the total population) still speak an indigenous language, and only a tenth (1.2 percent of total population) do not speak Spanish.

The largest Indian group are the Náhuatls, who number over 2.5 million. The Náhuatls are descended from the Aztecs. The Mayans, with a population of around 2.4 million, are the next largest group. There are also about 770,000 Zapotecs, 720,000 Mixtecs, and 400,000 Totonacs. These are descended from the better-known pre-Spanish civilizations.

Other large groups include the Otomís, the Mazahuas, the Huastecs, the Tzotzils, the Tzeltals, and the Huichols. Some groups, such as the Lacandons, the Kiliwas, the Cucapas, and the Paispais, have been reduced to a few dozen families. Most have absorbed aspects of mestizo culture, but a few still live in almost total isolation.

A mestizo family in Mexico. Mestizos are people of Spanish and Indian heritage.

Some remote Indian villages are cut off from many modern facilities, such as telephones and electricity. The lives of these villagers have remained virtually unchanged since the arrival of the Spanish. Many Indians still sleep on thin straw mats or in hammocks. Their villages form a striking contrast to the developed, cosmopolitan districts of Mexico City, Monterrey, and Guadalajara.

MESTIZOS

In contrast to the early European colonists of what became the United States and Canada, who brought entire families to the New World to start a new life, the Spanish conquerors were adventurers out to claim new lands for themselves and the Spanish crown. There was no place for women or children in their often-warlike adventures, so they left their families in Spain. Many of them married Indian women and settled in the colonies. Children born to these Spanish-Indian couples became the first mestizos.

Today 60 percent of the Mexican population is mestizo. No other former Spanish colony in Latin America is as thoroughly mestizo as Mexico. Large Indian populations still exist in Central and South America, but the ruling classes are usually made up of pure-blooded Europeans.

Although the colonies of other countries in the region were similarly shaped by migrants from Europe and later by slaves from Africa, only in Mexico did complete religious, political, and ethnic mixing take place.

TRADITIONAL DRESS

In the cities and large towns, Mexicans wear clothing similar to that worn in the United States. Village wear, however, is very simple and practical, designed to meet the needs of a particular region and climate. Often the designs are hundreds of years old.

In central and southern Mexico, village men usually wear plain cotton shirts and pants and leather sandals called huaraches. Wide-brimmed felt or straw hats called sombreros offer protection against the sun, and ponchos protect them from the rain. At night, men wrap themselves in serapes, colorful shawls hung over one shoulder during the day.

Local men in traditional wear at Tulum.

Village women wear blouses and long, full skirts and usually go barefoot. They use shawls called rebozos to cover their heads. Mothers also use rebozos to secure their babies on their backs.

Mexican Indians are famous for their beautiful homemade fabrics. Weaving styles differ throughout Mexico, and it is possible to identify an Indian's regional homeland by the color and design of his poncho or serape.

Some Indians have traditional clothing that is usually worn on holidays or for other celebrations. Indians in Oaxaca wear large straw capes. Women on the Isthmus of Tehuantepec wear a wide, lacy white headdress called a *huipil grande* (wee-PEEL GRAHN-day) on holidays. Mayan women in the Yucatán wear long, loose white dresses embroidered around the neck and bottom hem.

Perhaps the best known of all traditional Indian clothing is the *China poblana* (CHEE-nah poh-BLAH-nah). Worn by women, usually when performing the Mexican hat dance, it consists of a full red-and-green skirt decorated with beads and other ornaments; a short-sleeve, colorfully embroidered blouse; and a brightly colored sash.

POPULATION PROBLEMS

Mexico is home to more than 112 million people. Except for Brazil, it is the most populous country south of the Rio Grande. The Mexican population doubled between 1960 and 1980, largely due to improved health care for the poor. Beginning in 1930 the government introduced effective methods of treating childhood diseases in Mexico's poorer areas. Consequently more children survived to adulthood. People still thought many of their children would die young, however, so they continued to have large families, especially because the Catholic Church frowned on birth control.

Due in part to the education of birth control in 1976, the rate of population growth dropped from 3.5 percent before 1980 to 1.5 percent in 2000 and 1.1 percent in 2011. Also, people began to realize that more of their children had a chance of surviving to adulthood, so they started having fewer babies.

Another challenge for modern Mexico is the uneven distribution of resources such as health care, education, and land, causing the average Mexican standard of living to vary greatly among the economic classes.

IMMIGRANTS AND EMIGRANTS

Apart from Spanish colonizers, many other Europeans immigrated to Mexico during the late 19th century, including people from Britain, Ireland, Italy, France, and the Netherlands. In the early 20th century, immigrants also came from Turkey, Lebanon, China, and Korea. During the 1970s and 1980s, Mexico also opened its doors to refugees fleeing political persecution or economic hardship in other parts of Latin America, especially Argentina, Chile, Cuba, and Venezuela. The Argentine community in Mexico is estimated to be at about 30,000 people.

Sharing a border with the United States, Mexico is also where the largest number of American citizens have chosen to live abroad. It has been estimated that as many as a million Americans live in Mexico. Some are there for business, especially after the opening up of trade with NAFTA, whereas many others have chosen to retire to Mexico. The attractions are obvious: a lower cost of living, a relaxed lifestyle, and a good climate. Baja California and Mexico City are home to the greatest number of foreigners.

The movement of people has not been all one way, however: In 2000 as many as 20 million American residents identified themselves as either Mexican or of Mexican descent. This movement of people north of the border began after World War II, when factories in the United States started to recruit workers from Mexico. The migration grew rapidly during the 1990s drinksand first decade of the 21st century, with work and a better quality of life being the main draw. In 2008 there were 11.4 million Mexican immigrants in the United States (roughly 10 percent of the Mexican population), accounting for 30.1 percent of all U.S. immigrants.

Mexican immigrants mainly settle in "traditional" destination states such as California and Texas, although in recent years they have started to settle in southern states, such as North Carolina and Georgia, as well as Midwestern locations, such as Nebraska. As many as half of these immigrants were undocumented residents, prepared to flout the law to earn higher wages and make a better life for themselves and their families.

INTERNET LINKS

http://migration.ucdavis.edu/mn/more.php?id=3022_0_2_0

This website analyzes migration patterns and remittances from Mexican migrants in the United States during the past 20 years.

www.focusonmexico.com/gallery.aspx?tid=303

This website provides a selection of photographs of typical Mexicans.

http://studenttravel.about.com/od/mexicophotogalleries/ig/Mexico/

This website includes a collection of photographs of Mexican people going about their daily lives.

www.webexhibits.org/calendars/calendar-mayan.html

This website includes a detailed description of the Mayan calendar, with photographs.

LIFESTYLE

Pedestrians at the intersection of Paseo de la Reforma and
Eje Central Lázaro Cárdenas in Mexico City.

7

THERE IS A VERY BIG DIFFERENCE between city life and village life in Mexico. Most Mexican cities are cosmopolitan, with inhabitants who lead lifestyles similar to those led by people living in many cities in Europe and the United States. Values are generally more liberal in Mexico's urban areas than in the villages.

Traditionally most Mexicans lived in villages and worked the land. Today, however, three-quarters of Mexicans live an urban life in towns and cities.

The Plaza Paraiso Mall in Cabo San Lucas, Baja California.

Unidos para progresar   Solidaridad

GOBIERNO CONSTITU

San Juan Chamula in Mexico is famous for its cooperative market and traditional church.

Women have far more opportunities to pursue higher education in the cities, jobs are easier to find, and health care is more accessible. In contrast, life on farms and in villages has changed very little during the past century. Many farmers live in small villages near their fields. Still following ancient customs and living as their ancestors did before the Spanish arrived, some Indian villagers resent the imposition of mestizo culture.

A large number of Mexican cities and towns began as Indian communities. After the Spaniards conquered Mexico, they rebuilt the communities and made them more like Spanish towns. The central church and the main public and government buildings were built around a public square called a plaza. The plazas were meant to serve as the center of city life, much as they do in Europe.

In addition to a plaza, almost every village, city, and town in Mexico has a marketplace. Going to the market is an important activity for people in rural areas. Men, women, and children take whatever they wish to sell or trade and either rent stalls at which to display their goods or simply spread their merchandise on the ground. Then they spend the day at the market visiting with friends or selling their wares.

In the cities, affluent people often go to the mall in their free time. Generally the shops and department stores in the malls are open seven days a week, opening later in the morning to stay open later into the night; they often stay open later still on the weekends.

FAMILY: THE CORE OF SOCIETY

Mexican families form the core of the country's social structure. Indeed, the strength of the family forms the foundation of Mexico's continued political stability.

The Mexican family includes both immediate family and extended family—aunts, uncles, grandparents, and cousins. Families are extremely self-sufficient and closed to outsiders, except for very close friends who are considered part of the family. The family provides emotional and economic support to each of its members. Family-run farms, stores, shops, restaurants, and other businesses together employ millions of people. Even the poorest families offer their members more economic security in times of hardship than the government does. Many Mexican households are home to three, or maybe four, generations of the same family.

The social life of family members revolves around being with relatives. Children have so many brothers, sisters, and cousins that they may not need to play with other friends.

The Mexican family structure has survived a great deal of change in the past 40 years. More of the rural population have been forced to migrate to the cities in search of work. Children of middle-class and wealthy families have begun learning foreign languages and adopting foreign customs and are traveling much more than their parents ever did. Industrialization and urbanization have drastically changed provincial lifestyles. The Catholic Church has lost much of its influence as people have become less religious. But through it all, the family unit has survived. More than 90 percent of Mexicans still live in some kind of family group.

The average Mexican household consists of five or six people. Often several generations of the same family live together. The head of the family is often the grandfather or the great-grandfather. The father is the unquestioned figure of authority. Unfortunately, sometimes his job or his machismo leads him to neglect his wife and family. Also, he typically feels that maintaining the home is solely the woman's duty. A mother is usually adored by her children, as she is the one who gives them all the care and attention.

The average Mexican family consists of at least five or six members, the father being the breadwinner and usually the head of the family. Older sisters often help their mother look after younger siblings.

STAGES OF LIFE

CHILDHOOD AND ADOLESCENCE

Mexican girls do not have nearly as much freedom as girls in the United States. Peasant girls are assigned household chores from the time they are very young, and by the time they are seven or eight, most are helping to care for their younger brothers and sisters. In Mexican villages, little girls can often be seen carrying their baby brothers or sisters on their backs.

Rural peasants think of cities as sinful places and are extremely reluctant to allow their daughters to move to the cities. The only possible exception would be if the girl could move in with a relative who has already settled in the city.

Mexican boys are usually doted on by their mothers. Unlike girls, boys are allowed more independence and free time, as they are not expected to do household chores. In the villages, though, sons normally help in the fields.

In both villages and cities, most young men and women live at home until they are married. Many children of wealthy families live and study abroad. Yet upon their return, they go back to their parents' home.

MARRIAGE Marriage, rather than cohabitation, is still the norm in Mexico, and most people expect to get married. Mexican weddings are large, noisy affairs, where every member of both the bride's and the groom's extended families is invited to celebrate. A lasso or a large rosary is symbolically draped around the neck or shoulders of the groom and then of the bride, tying them together. It affirms the couple's commitment to always be together. The couple wears the lasso throughout the service, and at the end of the ceremony it is removed and given to the bride as a keepsake. Another interesting tradition is the money dance, where male guests pay to dance with the bride. This money becomes part of the couple's wedding gift.

Sisters manning their family's fruit store at a market in San Christóbal de las Casas in Chiapas. It is common for young girls to help with family work, especially in the home or in the family business.

Marriage in Indian villages is still very traditional. Village girls usually marry between ages 14 and 16, and village boys in their late teens. Marriages are still arranged in some Indian communities, and the bride's family is expected to pay a dowry. Huichol girls marry when they are as young as 13. Men commonly have more than one wife, and adultery is tolerated in men.

In the rural southeast, custom requires that the male members of the family object to a woman's leaving home. Thus she is often taken forcefully by her boyfriend, with peace eventually being restored between the families only after the couple's first child is born.

Poor Indians usually cannot afford a marriage license but still live together as husband and wife. These marriages are considered valid in the eyes of their peers. Some Indians wear feathers of small birds in their hair to indicate that they are married.

PREGNANCY AND CHILDBIRTH Birth control is not widely practiced in Mexico, and many women become pregnant shortly after getting married. If an unmarried village girl becomes pregnant, the father of her child will usually marry her. This is not necessarily the case, however, in the cities, and the number of unwed mothers is much higher in the urban areas than in the villages.

A funeral in procession. People believe that the spirit or soul of a person never dies.

DEATH AND FUNERALS Mexicans celebrate the Day of the Dead every November with picnics at the cemetery. They eat on the graves of their ancestors, believing that departed souls return on that day. Many Mexicans believe the living can communicate with the dead. To them, the past is never dead, and death is not the end but a phase in an infinite cycle.

The Mexican view of death goes back to the religion of the Aztecs and the influence of the Catholic missionaries. The Aztecs believed the death of a sacrificial victim had special significance, and they offered human sacrifices to please the gods. By contrast, the Catholic missionaries believed that what happened to the individual after death depended on how he or she had lived.

WOMEN

Although women in Mexico are generally treated as subordinate to men, their role in society is crucial. Despite the bravado of Mexican machismo, Mexican women are the pillars of the family. Mothers pass on to their children religious beliefs, myths and legends, and customs and traditions that form the foundation of family and community life.

The Mexican attitude toward women is less liberal than that of the United States and northern Europe. In Mexico a woman's principal assets are thought to be beauty, compassion, and tenderness. She is expected to obey her husband and provide him with pleasure, assistance, and counsel. She is expected to always treat him with respect, as he is the one who supports and protects her.

As in most other Latin American countries, peasant women in Mexico do very little outside the home besides going to the market. At home, they

MACHISMO

Machismo *refers to the strong sense of masculine pride felt by many Mexican men. They constantly try to prove their manhood by, for example, having mistresses, being domineering and overly protective of women around them, paying the bill in restaurants even if they cannot afford it, and having many children to demonstrate their fertility. They feel they must be aggressive and project an image of strength.*

Many Mexicans think, however, that machismo is a front men put up to hide their insecurities. Mexican men often try to cover up their fears with ostentatious displays of manliness, and it is believed they do this mainly to impress other men.

But the most damaging effects of machismo on Mexican society may be manifested in the adulterous habits of married men and in the way they treat women. Machismo has

been a contributing factor in the breakdown of many marriages and in the occurrence of many pregnancies, which partly explains the country's high birthrate.

Machismo has not been all bad, however. Being macho has not prevented Mexican men from being gentle with children and affectionate toward friends, and even the most macho of men may cry in public.

prepare the food, wash the clothes, and raise the children. They usually have many children, not only because birth control is difficult to obtain but also because they need the extra hands to help with the work. In addition, having many children ensures that they will have someone to provide for them when they grow old. Traditional husbands also believe it is important to produce many children to show their masculinity.

Peasant women rarely talk to strangers and never join their husbands in entertaining visitors. The only exception may be grandmothers, especially those whose husbands have died. Grandmothers are revered and so may do "unfeminine" things in public, such as drinking and smoking.

A family portrait of three generations of Mexican women in Oaxaca.

In urban areas, middle-class and wealthy women have much more freedom than those from poorer families. Economic conditions have made it necessary for more women to go to work. Official statistics suggest that women make up a quarter of the workforce, although unofficially the figure may be much higher. Women tend to have jobs when they are younger, between the ages of 20 and 25. After this time, they often stop work to raise a family. However, while the vast majority of Mexico's working women continue to be single, it is becoming much more acceptable for married women with children to work. There has also been a steady increase in the number of women attending universities, which has enabled them to find higher-income jobs in the public and private sectors.

CUSTOMS

GREETINGS AND FAREWELLS In Mexico greetings and goodbyes are quite warm and affectionate and always involve a handshake. Women kiss each other on the cheek when introduced and whenever they meet. These formalities are very important, and it is considered rude to ignore them. The main form of greeting, especially between men, is the *abrazo* (AH-bre-so). It follows a strict pattern. First comes the handshake, followed by the embrace and two strong coordinated pats on the back, and finally, a second handshake and a pat on the shoulder.

COMPADRE* AND *COMADRE Literally these words translate as "cofather" and "comother" and refer to the godfather and the godmother of one's children. *Compadres* (kohm-PAH-drays) and *comadres* (koh-MAH-drays) often support each other in times of need.

Younger men sometimes call their close friends *compadre*. Although this is often done in a casual manner, in some cases it carries the connotation that they feel so close to a certain friend that they would gladly welcome him into their family as the godfather of a son or a daughter.

Modern college friends making their way down the steps together.

THE *MAÑANA* SYNDROME Mexicans, along with other Latin Americans in general, have their own unique sense of time; they like to live in the present. Many believe that if a task is not an absolute emergency, it can probably be put off until tomorrow. This attitude, called *mañana* (mah-NYAH-nah), can be very frustrating to people who are unfamiliar with it. Mexicans can be hours late for appointments or not show up at all. They believe anything being enjoyed at the moment is not worth ending for the sake of a serious appointment.

It is also difficult for Mexicans to say no. They may accept invitations and make appointments that they have no intention of keeping because they believe it is ruder to refuse an invitation than to not show up for it. This attitude is called the *mañana* syndrome.

POLITENESS Mexicans are very polite. When asked, "Where are you from?" they will often answer "*Donde tiene su casa*" or "Where your home is," implying that "my home is your home."

One must be careful when admiring another's possessions. The owner of the item often will offer it to the admirer as a gift. Envy is a discouraged emotion among Mexicans.

SIESTAS Most Mexicans living in villages and rural areas eat a big meal called *comida* (koh-MEE-dah) in the afternoon and possibly take a nap, or

Some colorful and unique houses are found in the colonial town of Guanajuato, listed as a World Heritage Site by UNESCO.

siesta, until about 4 P.M. During this time, shops close and things become very quiet. Schoolchildren also go home for a siesta and resume classes in the afternoon. In cities, hectic schedules and conventional business hours are steadily eliminating the siesta custom.

SOCIAL CONDITIONS

Wealthy Mexican citizens lead lifestyles comparable to those of the elite of any country. Mexico also has a fairly large, comfortable middle class. However, the majority of the population, consisting mostly of mestizos and indigenous people, live in poverty, some barely making ends meet. Mexico is formally committed to improving social conditions; the government spends billions of dollars annually on social welfare programs.

HEALTH Although improving social assistance and health services has greatly reduced Mexico's death rate during the past 70 years, the health of the rural and urban poor is still far below the government's minimum standards. Malnutrition is common and is the cause of many diseases, such as rickets and anemia. There are also many cases of tonsillitis, influenza, and respiratory diseases. The average life span in Mexico is about 79 years for women and 73 years for men (compared with 81 years for women and 76 years for men in the United States).

HOUSING A shortage of housing, particularly in the cities, is one of the most serious of Mexico's social problems. There is also the problem of poor housing, which the government has sought to address. Today 96 percent of urban households and 73 percent of rural homes have running water supply, compared with less than 50 percent in 1990. Sanitation has also improved hugely over the same period.

EDUCATION Since the 1910 revolution, Mexico has invested large amounts of money in its education system, successfully helping many Mexicans improve their lives. But the growing population creates new problems for the education system, since more schools and teachers are required. Almost all Mexicans attend preschool and primary school, but only 70 percent go on to secondary education and roughly a quarter to higher education. Almost 15 percent of Mexican adults are illiterate.

WAGES AND COST OF LIVING The average Mexican man works from dawn to dusk. However, he is paid low wages and often does not earn enough to feed or house his family properly. As a result, many women and children have to do odd jobs to supplement the family income. Average annual income in Mexico is around $13,000, although wealth is unevenly spread, so many people earn much less than this, while a few earn much more.

Students study in the Central Library at the National Autonomous University of Mexico in Mexico City.

A law introduced in 1934 requires employers to pay their employees at least the minimum wage. This law, however, is rarely observed. In any case, the minimum wage is not enough to support a family, as it is 57 pesos a day, which adds up to barely $2,000 a year. Workers are entitled to ask for a raise twice a year, but the typical increase in wages rarely covers the increase in cost of living. Almost 20 percent of Mexicans were considered to live below the poverty line in 2010.

CASA MEXICANA

Mexican suburbs are full of modern houses and apartment buildings, the homes of Mexico's expanding middle class. The older parts of the cities have

MEXICO CITY

Mexico City, the capital of Mexico, is one of the largest cities in the world, with an estimated population of around 20 million. The city was founded soon after the Spanish conquest, on the site of Tenochtitlán, the Aztec capital. The city has a colorful history. Before independence, Mexico City was the capital of New Spain. The city was captured by U.S. troops during the Mexican-American War (1846—48) and was briefly held by the French army in 1863. The city was later captured by Mexican rebel forces during the Mexican Revolution in 1910.

Mexico City always surprises visitors with its sophistication and European air. It is a culturally rich, dynamic city full of Aztec ruins, colonial buildings, beautiful parks, superb shopping malls, and excellent museums. On the other hand, some of the poorest Mexicans live in Mexico City. Also, the city has developed a critical pollution problem in recent years. The millions of cars, trucks, and buses swarming the city produce pollutants that are easily trapped in the bowl-shaped valley where Mexico City is located.

rows of Spanish colonial-style homes. Most of these houses are made of stone or adobe brick and have patios located at the center of the house. These patios served as the center of life for the Spanish families who inhabited these houses.

Poorer Mexicans live in slum shacks or rooms with almost no furniture. *Petates* (pay-TAH-tays), or straw mats, serve as beds. Clay bowls serve as dishes. An entire family may live in a one-room house. The shapes, styles, and building materials of these homes vary according to the requirements of the climate. Homes on the dry central plateau are made of adobe, cement, or stone, with flat roofs of red tiles, sheet metal, or straw. Some have hard-packed dirt floors, one door, and few or no windows. Cooking is done on a stove placed against an outside wall or over a fire on the floor.

In areas with heavy rainfall, most houses have walls made of poles covered with a mixture of lime and clay. This mixture lasts longer in the rain than adobe does. The houses have sloping roofs. In Yucatán, most Indian houses are rectangular in shape but have rounded corners. Roofs are made of neatly trimmed palm leaves.

Mañana is a Spanish word meaning "tomorrow." A *mañana* attitude prevails in many Spanish-speaking cultures.

INTERNET LINKS

www.mexconnect.com/regions?type=Gallery

This website includes hundreds of photos of Mexicans from all walks of life and in a variety of settings.

www.facts-about-mexico.com/mexican-christmas.html

This website features an article that explains the special characteristics of a Mexican Christmas.

www.kwintessential.co.uk/articles/article/Mexico/Mexican-Family-Traditions/1073

This website describes Mexican family traditions, with links to articles on the family at Christmas, weddings, and traditional clothing.

RELIGION

The interior of Our Lady of Guadalupe Cathedral in Puerto Vallarta, Jalisco.

8

ACCORDING TO the last official census, carried out in 2000, 76.5 percent of Mexicans were Roman Catholic, whereas 6.3 percent were Protestant (including Pentecostals and Jehovah's Witnesses). Mexico has no official religion, and the constitution of 1917 limits the church from getting involved in politics.

Mexico recognizes all the major religions, and Mexicans are free to worship whichever faith they please. There are small populations of Muslims and Jews in Mexico, and Mormons (members of the Church of Jesus Christ of Latter-day Saints) number more than 200,000.

Like most of Latin America, Mexico is a predominantly Roman Catholic country, with the second-largest Catholic population in the world, after Brazil.

The iconic La Parroquia de San Miguel Arcáangel Church in San Miguel de Allende.

NATIVE RELIGION

The first Indians in Mexico were probably hunter-gatherers from Asia who crossed the Bering Strait tens of thousands of years ago. When changes in climate killed off their food source, they were forced to cultivate the land. Agriculture became so important to them that they began worshiping gods who they believed would provide rain and protect their harvests.

The indigenous people worshiped many gods. Each of these gods controlled a different aspect of life and had its own personality, kind or cruel. Some Indian groups believed that their gods required human sacrifice as a payment for granting them favors, so they built temples to honor the gods.

A Tarahumara Indian shaman woman holding a rite to purify people from evil forces.

ARRIVAL OF CATHOLICISM

After the Spanish conquest, Catholic missionaries came to Mexico from Spain to convert the Indians to Christianity. The missionaries were often sent to remote villages. Converting the Indians was not difficult, because of certain similarities between Catholicism and indigenous religions.

Realizing they had a better chance of succeeding if they compromised, the missionaries allowed the Indians to keep some of their own religious traditions. They also built churches on or near Indian temples, often destroying the temples and using the same stones to build the churches. The indigenous population began to worship many Catholic saints as Indian deities, thus creating a religious system combining Christian and Indian beliefs. In urban areas, Indian culture was eventually overrun by European culture, and indigenous beliefs disappeared.

ANTI-CHURCH REFORMS

From the time of the Spanish conquest, the Catholic Church was regarded with some suspicion by mestizos and Indians. Although some early priests tried to protect the Indians, many clergymen exploited the indigenous population. During the War of Independence, the Catholic Church, afraid of losing its power, backed the pro-Spanish conservatives. In response, the new government after independence began enacting anti-Catholic laws. Many of these laws were passed during the presidency of Benito Juárez. The 1910 revolution further restricted the Catholic Church.

The constitution of 1917 contains many reforms that limit the power of the Catholic Church. A man and a woman must marry in a civil court before they can have a religious ceremony. Land and buildings that once belonged to the Catholic Church are now state property. No church leader is allowed to make a political statement in public. Priests are not allowed to vote or to wear their clerical robes in public. The government also limits the number of men who can become priests, and these are restricted to local-born Mexicans.

THE CHURCH TODAY

Despite their best efforts, the Spanish missionaries were not able to destroy all Indian beliefs. Nature, magic, and mystery remain an important part of indigenous religions. Some Indians living in remote villages still worship their ancestral gods, but most Mexicans practice a form of Catholicism that incorporates elements of Indian faiths.

In 2002 Pope John Paul II visited Mexico for the fifth time. Hundreds of thousands of people flocked to see him. Although the papal visits strengthened Catholicism in Mexico, the Catholic Church has lost much of its influence on the lives of Mexicans. Although most Mexicans are Catholic, evangelical groups are growing rapidly. Currently 6 percent of the Mexican population is Protestant, including almost a half-million Seventh-Day Adventists and up to 2 million Jehovah's Witnesses. Church attendance among Catholics, especially in urban areas, is dropping, as is the ratio of priests to population. Recent statistics suggest that just 3 percent of Mexicans attend church regularly.

THE VIRGIN OF GUADALUPE

There is a fervent and widespread belief in Mexico in the miracle of the Virgin of Guadalupe.

According to legend, in 1531 a poor Indian named Juan Diego saw the Virgin of Guadalupe on his way to church, one day after he had converted to Catholicism. She appeared as an Indian maiden on Tepeyac Hill at La Villa, just outside Mexico City. She asked Diego to tell the local bishop to build a shrine in her honor on the hill, so that she could protect the Indians. The bishop, however, did not believe Diego's story.

The next day, the Virgin appeared again. When Diego told the bishop about this, he demanded proof. When the Virgin appeared a third time, Diego told her about the bishop's request for proof. She told him to collect roses from a spot on the hill where roses had never grown before. Diego wrapped the roses in a blanket and brought them to the

bishop. When he unwrapped the parcel, they both saw the image of the Virgin imprinted on the inside of the blanket. The bishop then built the shrine and placed the cloth in it. The Basilica of the Virgin of Guadalupe was rebuilt in 1976. The construction was financed by the government, a remarkable gesture considering its official anti-Church stance. The government's involvement in the building of the church indicates the importance of the Virgin to Mexicans. The Virgin of Guadalupe had become a symbol of the Mexican nation by the time of the Mexican War of Independence in 1820. The armies of both Miguel Hidalgo in 1810 and Emiliano Zapata in 1914 flew Guadalupan flags. Today the Virgin of Guadalupe remains a strong national and religious symbol in Mexico.

In 2002 Juan Diego was canonized in the Basilica of the Virgin of Guadalupe by Pope John Paul II before a crowd of 12 million people.

Divorce is becoming more socially acceptable, and many people use birth control, which runs against Catholic teachings. Abortion is a fairly common practice and was legalized in some Mexican states in 2007, despite opposition from the Catholic Church and Pope Benedict XVI.

Despite the law forbidding non-Mexican priests, there are many foreign priests in Mexico due to the shortage of local-born priests. Though Church leaders at times publicly speak out against the government, most priests keep a low profile.

While laws restricting the Church's influence used to be strictly enforced, they have become more relaxed today. The voting population is overwhelmingly Catholic, so some political leaders try to get around enforcing the rules to attract more votes.

Although the Church as an institution has weakened over the years, religious beliefs are still an integral part of Mexican life. Village priests are often powerful community leaders, and husband—wife relationships are still based on the teachings of the Bible and the Church.

INTERNET LINKS

www.inside-mexico.com/featuresemana.htm

This website offers a description and photographs of Holy Week in Mexico.

www.bluffton.edu/~sullivanm/mexico/mexicocity/cathedral/cathedral.html

This is a site showing the Metropolitan Cathedral in Mexico City from every angle, with descriptions.

http://latino.si.edu/Mexican%20Treasures/english/religion_festivals.html

This website shows artifacts and describes the religious rituals of Mexico's ancient native cultures.

LANGUAGE

Mexican college students read, write, and speak Spanish.

9

M OST MEXICANS SPEAK SPANISH, the dominant language of most Latin American countries. With 112 million people, Mexico has the largest Spanish-speaking population in the world. However, there are still small numbers of Indians living in remote areas in Mexico who do not speak Spanish.

MEXICAN SPANISH

The Spanish spoken in Mexico is different from the Spanish spoken in Spain, somewhat the way the English spoken in the United States is different from the English spoken in Great Britain. Mexican Spanish is a hybrid of Spanish, Indian languages, and some English.

"Stop" is translated as *alto* in Spanish.

A classroom in a village school. The Mexican government has set up schools where Spanish is taught to Indian students in an effort to integrate them into mainstream society and help them improve their economic status.

Even within Mexico, there are differences in the way people speak Mexican Spanish. People from the *tierra fría*, the highlands, tend to speak slowly and enunciate every word, whereas people living in the *tierra caliente*, the tropical zones, speak faster and often drop the ending sound of words, particularly if the words end in the letter *s*.

Mexicans prefer to speak indirectly to avoid confrontation or commitment. This has led to remarkable creativity in the Mexican use of Spanish. Many words have double meanings that would not be understood by people who are not familiar with the connotations. Excessive frankness or directness is considered rude, and even serious discussions must be preceded by political gossip or small talk about family.

Many words used in English are of Mexican-Spanish origin, such as *canyon*, *corral*, *desperado*, *lasso*, *patio*, *rodeo*, and *stampede*.

INDIAN LANGUAGES

In 2003 the Mexican congress approved the General Law of Linguistic Rights of Indigenous Peoples, which recognized Mexico's native languages with the same status and validity as Spanish. While millions of Mexican Indians speak their indigenous languages on a daily basis, the vast majority are also fluent in Spanish. Around 7 percent of the population can speak a native language. The most widely spoken Indian language in Mexico is Náhuatl, the language of the Aztecs, followed by the Mixtec, Mayan, Zapotec, and Otomi languages. These languages are different from one another, with very few common words among them.

It is estimated that there are 62 Indian languages in Mexico today, in addition to numerous minor dialects. Some of these dialects—for example, Aguacatec—are spoken by only a few individuals or groups.

The Spanish thought they could accelerate Indian integration into colonial society by eliminating indigenous languages. Although attempts by

COMMISSION FOR THE DEFENSE OF SPANISH

Over the years, the government of Mexico has tried very hard to maintain its cultural independence from the United States. In the early 1980s the government noticed that more and more English words were creeping into the Spanish language. For example, people were calling themselves Charlie instead of Carlos, or Paul instead of Pablo. Owners of restaurants and shops, thinking foreign words fashionable and good for business, began giving their establishments English names, such as Shirley's and Arthur's.

In 1982 the government created the Commission for the Defense of the Spanish Language. The commission's purpose was to prevent English from becoming mixed with the Spanish language. It declared war on the apostrophe—which does not exist in Spanish—as the principal symbol of cultural mixing. The commission also made radio and television commercials that mocked people using English phrases. The commission's impact has been slight, however, and English words from the United States continue to gain currency in Mexico.

the Spanish to wipe out Indian languages from Mexico were not completely successful, it is estimated that as many as 93 Indian languages have disappeared since the Spanish conquest.

Government policy no longer forces the Spanish language on the Indians. For instance, when the government began a war against illiteracy in 1944, it provided Indians with important information in their own languages, though written in Roman script. These communications enabled the Indians to learn about the advantages of learning Spanish, such as the ability to improve their education and economic condition. Television and radio, which broadcast mainly in Spanish, were added incentives for Indians to learn the language. Most Indians have become part of the Spanish-speaking community while keeping their distinct culture and traditions.

HEY, AMIGO!

FORMALITIES AND TITLES Mexicans have two ways of saying "you." *Tú* (too) is the familiar form, used when talking to friends. *Usted* (oos-TED) is

The top 10 Indian languages by number of speakers are Náhuatl, 1,376,026; Yucatec Maya, 759,000; Mixtec, 423,216; Zapotec, 410,901; Tzeltal Maya, 371,730; Tzotzil Maya, 329,937; Otomi, 239,850; Totonac, 230,930; Mazatec, 206,559; Ch'ol (Mayan), 185,299

1. *Ojo (OH-ho), or "eye," is a shrewd person's way of warning someone to be careful or to watch out.*

2. *¿Quién sabe? (KEE-en SAH-bay), or "Who knows?," is usually accompanied by raised eyebrows, facial contortions, and groans. It means "I take no responsibility."*

3. *Las uñas (lahs OO-nyas), or "fingernails," may refer to either a thief or a theft and is often used as a warning that a known thief is nearby or as a way of saying that something has been stolen.*

4. *This gesture is used to indicate the height of inanimate objects.*

5. *This gesture is used to indicate the height of animals.*

6. *This gesture is used to indicate the height of people. (It can be insulting to use gesture 4 or 5 when referring to people.)*

7. *Lana (LAH-nah), or "money," is a way of saying something is expensive.*

8. *¡Ijole! (ee-HOH-lay), or "Wow!" The fingers should make an audible pop.*

9. *No, ni modos (no, nee MOH-dohs), or "No, no way."*

10. *Adelante (ad-day-LAHN-tay), or "ahead," is a common gesture, though it can confuse Americans. It looks like "go away," but it means "come here" or "move forward."*

11. *Momentito, ahoritita (moh-men-TEE-toh, ah-or-ree-TEE-tah), or "a moment," means "not much," "a little bit," or even "I'll be right back." It is often used in place of a verbal promise that one knows cannot be fulfilled.*

12. *No, gracias (no, GRAH-see-ahs), or "No, thank you," is used in the same way as in the United States: as a sign of appreciation when turning something down.*

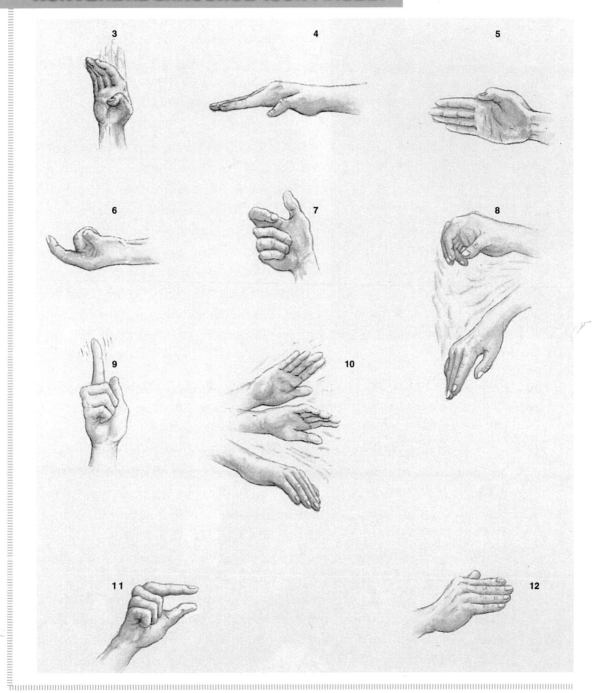

the formal form. Mexicans are very strict about when to use each form. It is considered impolite to use *tú* when greeting a stranger, an elder, or someone of a higher social status. In this case, *tutear* (too-teh-AHR), which means "to use the pronoun *tú*," is acceptable only after it has been agreed on by both parties.

NICKNAMES Nicknames are very common in Mexico and are often simply versions of proper names, as in *Tonio* from *Antonio*. Many others are derived from people's looks, personalities, or jobs. Someone who is overweight may be called *Gordo* (GOR-doh), or "Fatty," and someone with a broad nose might be nicknamed *Chato* (CHAH-toh), or "Pug Nose." *Junior* is an insulting nickname for those whose status comes from the power or money of their parents.

Students research on computers in a university in Mexico. The people residing in the city enjoy the use of technology and the Internet.

CLASS DIFFERENCES Although they deny the existence of racial discrimination, many upper-class Mexicans have developed a special vocabulary that indicates in a subtle way their position in society.

Wealthy Mexicans are called *gente de razón* (HEN-tay day rah-SOHN), or "people of reason." The opposite of the *gente de razón* are the *gente indígena* (een-DEE-hay-nah), or the Indians. Some mestizos call themselves *cristianosas* (kris-tee-ah-NOH-sahs) to indicate that they are not Indians. The poor, even if they are mestizo, are referred to as *indios* (EEN-dee-ohs) or *inditos* (een-DEE-tohs), which literally means "little Indians." This term, which mixes race with class, is considered an insult.

SLANG As it is elsewhere, this is an important method of communication in Mexico, which can be difficult to understand for those unfamiliar with it. For example, Mexicans refer to the United States as "the other side." They also call a car *la nave*, meaning "ship," and money *lana*, meaning "wool."

MALINCHISMO The Mexican word for "traitor," or one who rejects his own cultural heritage in favor of foreign things, is *malinchista* (mah-leen-CHEES-tah). It comes from the name of an Indian maiden, La Malinche, one of Hernán Cortés's translators and also his mistress. Through La Malinche, a princess named Malintzin who had been sold out of her tribe, Cortés was able to form alliances with Indians that aided the success of the Spanish conquest.

A newspaper vendor enjoying a quiet read.

INTERNET LINKS

www.rollybrook.com/pronunciation.htm

This is a clear guide to Mexican-Spanish pronunciation, sound by sound through the alphabet.

www.omniglot.com/writing/nahuatl.htm

This website provides a comprehensive account of the history, pronunciation, and alphabet for Náhuatl, the language of the Aztecs.

www.focusonmexico.com/News-and-Views/Articles/2009-Newsletters/August-Articles/Spanish-101-Pronunciation-and-Useful-Phrases.html

This is a brief guide to some popular Mexican words and phrases and how to pronounce them.

www.espanol-ingles.com.mx/mexican-spanish/

This useful website illustrates the difference between Peninsular (European) and Mexican Spanish, as well as offering an English translation of some popular phrases.

The Palacio de Bellas Artes (Palace of Fine Arts) is the most important cultural center in Mexico City as well as the rest of the country. Mexico has many fascinating museums that display its rich ancient history, strong artistic tradition, and cultural diversity.

10

MEXICAN ART AND ARCHITECTURE display a combination of cultural and social themes, such as the ancient Indian civilizations, Spanish colonialism, Catholicism, and the revolutionary ideas of 19th-century politics in Mexico.

Mexican indigenous art before the Spanish conquest had already achieved a remarkable level of development and sophistication. Created by Indians with virtually no outside influence, Mexican ancient art is valued not only for its artistic merit but also for its historical and archaeological importance.

Clay skeleton figures by local artisans on display for the Day of the Dead festival.

Mexico's artistic heritage is one of the oldest and richest in the Americas. The country's artistic history stretches back more than 3,000 years.

The Aztec Sunstone is a remarkable work of art and science. The Sunstone was used as a calendar to calculate the number of days in a year.

Indian groups managed to preserve their art and culture after the arrival of the Spaniards, but European styles gradually influenced Mexican writing, painting, music, and architecture. After the revolution, the country began to use its unique culture to promote a sense of national identity. Art became a powerful medium for patriotism.

Mexican art continues to draw inspiration from the country's colorful history and unique blend of Spanish and indigenous Mexican styles and themes. Nevertheless, in recent years, the artistic traditions of other countries have begun to put their mark on Mexican art, providing new freedom and inspiration for Mexican artists to develop new techniques.

MEXICAN INDIAN ART AND ARCHITECTURE

Most Mexican indigenous art before the arrival of the Spanish was inspired by religion. The gods of the indigenous people dominated every facet of Indian life, and many Indian works of art were created as offerings to the gods. The Olmecs, who between 1300 and 400 B.C. developed the first civilized culture in Mexico, were also the country's first artists. They made jewelry and ceramics but are best known for their stone carvings. Huge shapes of human heads, discovered mostly in the state of Veracruz, are the earliest portraits that remain of these ancient people. These heads are believed to have been created in honor of the Olmec rulers.

The Olmecs were the first civilization to build pyramids, an architectural style that would become important in every culture that followed. The Olmec pyramids began as mounds of earth covered with rough stones. They were later developed into beautiful, elaborate structures. The pyramids served

several functions. They were temples where priests could pray and perform rituals for the gods. They were also symbolic mountains meant to bring people closer to heaven. The Pyramid of the Niches in Tajín is one of the most magnificent in Mexico.

Later civilizations, such as the Mayans, continued to build magnificent cities and pyramids. The Mayan cities of Palenque, Chichén Itzá, and Uxmal display the Mayans' extraordinary artistic talent. The last indigenous Mexican empire, the Aztec, founded a magnificent capital, Tenochtitlán, on the site of present-day Mexico City. Teotihuacán, located to the northeast of Mexico City, is another fine example of an ancient Indian city, with extraordinary pyramids, temples, and roads made for the kings.

The Indians considered artistic skill a moral virtue and a way of expressing religious fervor. Their accomplishments are remarkable considering that they did not use iron tools. When the Spaniards arrived, they were impressed by the art and architecture of the Mexican Indians. The Spaniards also believed, however, that much of Mexican Indian art was the work of the devil. The Spaniards melted down gold objects, shattered sacred sculptures, and burned artifacts. Some objects have survived, and they have been safely put on display in museums around the country.

The Pyramid of the Niches is the focus of the El Tajín archaeological site.

MODERN ARCHITECTURE

After trying to wipe out pre-Columbian art forms, the Spanish taught the Indians to use European architectural and building techniques. The result was a new architectural style that combined European and indigenous forms.

The development of modern architecture in Mexico in many ways paralleled that of Mexican painting. Mexican architectural tradition, which began in pre-Spanish times, culminated during the rule of dictator Porfirio Díaz. President Díaz was responsible for building the Palace of Fine Arts and the congress building. During the 1920s architecture adjusted to the political mood of nationalism. The state constructed large buildings decorated with murals and sculptures, including the impressive Secretariat of Communications and Public Works in Mexico City. As with painting, Mexican architecture entered a creative period in the 1950s, achieving dramatic and exciting results by blending the colors and shapes of traditional Mexican art with modern styles and techniques imported from abroad. These projects include the impressive Ciudad Universitaria outside Mexico City, a complex of buildings and grounds housing the National Autonomous University of Mexico.

A young girl in her elaborately embroidered huipil.

CRAFTS AND FOLK ARTS

Crafts and folk arts have flourished throughout Mexican history, and despite increased modernization, they still make up a vital part of the nation's life and economy. When Mexicans eat, dress, play, or pray, they use replicas of the crafts used by their ancestors.

The making of contemporary Mexican crafts still follows ancient Indian traditions. As in pre-Spanish Mexico, pottery is a major activity, and much of it is still made by hand, without the use of a wheel. Weaving is still frequently done on a backstrap loom. *Huipils* (wee-peels), which are long embroidered dresses; long blouses; *quexquemetls* (KEX-kay-meh-tls), or ponchos; and capes worn in the past by Indian women are still woven today and worn on special occasions such as weddings and fiestas.

The revolution of 1910 had a dramatic effect on Mexican art. Artists began using patriotic and political themes in their work and realistic styles to depict contemporary political conflicts. The revolution also inspired a group of young painters to search for a style that would incorporate the great art of the indigenous people, as they felt that their art should be a reflection of the common people in Mexico. These artists specialized in painting large murals in public buildings. Three leaders of the Mexican muralist movement were Diego Rivera, David Siqueiros, and José Orozco. Together they transformed the art world of their time and place.

Mexican muralism was an art movement founded by Rivera during the 1930s. Inspired by indigenous Mexican art and his experiences in Europe, he painted murals dealing with Mexican history and society. Siqueiros was a political activist. He fought in the Mexican Revolution, volunteered to fight in the Spanish Civil War of the 1930s, and took part in labor struggles. Having been imprisoned on several occasions, he made social unrest the focus of his paintings. Orozco is considered the best Mexican muralist of all time. While Rivera and Siqueiros were noted also for their work in easel painting and sculpture, Orozco was at his best painting murals (below). His work reflects strong political feelings and a search for deep and universal symbols.

A traditional mariachi band playing their music as they walk down the streets.

The Spanish influence on Mexican crafts has been significant. Wool was unknown in ancient Mexico until sheep were introduced into the Americas. Serapes, rebozos (scarfs), and artistic techniques such as glazing are evidence of the Spanish influence.

MUSIC

Music was a very important part of the culture of Mexico's early Indians. They believed that music kept the world in motion and controlled natural phenomena. All Indian ceremonies involved music. Indigenous Mexicans also used music to teach children about their history and traditions.

Indigenous Mexicans played whistles, flutes, percussion instruments, drums, giant conch shells, rattles, trumpets, and notched deer bones. The earliest remaining musical instruments date from about 1500 B.C. and were made of bone, wood, animal hide, or baked clay.

The Spanish conquistadores tried to destroy Indian music, which they thought was inspired by the devil. Their efforts failed, partly because Spanish priests found it easier to convert the Indians if they allowed the Indians to transfer the use of traditional ceremonial music from the worship of pagan deities to the honoring of Catholic saints. Indians in some parts of Mexico still play the music of their ancestors.

MUSEO NACIONAL DE ANTROPOLOGÍA

The Museo Nacional de Antropología (National Museum of Anthropology) is one of the most outstanding museums in the Americas. Located in Mexico City, the museum is home to Mexican art, architecture, ethnography, and artifacts from 1700 B.C. to the Spanish conquest. The museum building was designed in 1963 and has an impressive architecture, with 23 exhibition halls and rooms surrounding a patio with a huge pond and a vast square concrete umbrella. Rooms and halls are dedicated to the main civilizations and periods in Mexican history, including preclassical, Teotihuacán, Toltec, Oaxaca, Gulf of Mexico, and Mayan.

The highlights of the museum include a full-scale reproduction of the Temple of Quetzalcóatl at Teotihuacán; the Ocelotl-Cuauhxicalli, a model of a jaguar with a hollow in its back in which human hearts were placed; a model of Xochipilli, the god of love, poetry, and dance; a reproduction of the Royal Tomb at Palenque; and the Olmec colossal heads, dating back to 1200 B.C., which puzzlingly appear to have African-style features, although they were produced in a period before America had any contact with Africa.

A popular style of Mexican music is the *norteña* (nor-TAY-nyah), which combines the tunes of *corridos* (coh-REE-dos), or Mexican ballads, with waltzes and polkas. These dances were brought to Mexico by thousands of Eastern European and German immigrants who settled in the country in the mid-1800s.

Son (soñé) is a type of traditional music developed from Spanish, native, and African influences. *Son* covers a whole range of styles, including zapateado (foot-stamping dance) and mariachi. *Son* musicians have to be able to improvise dances and lyrics in response to comments or requests from the dance floor.

Yaqui Indians performing the deer dance in Mexico.

The musicians most associated with Mexico are the mariachis. Mariachi bands consist of anywhere from three to more than a dozen musicians who wear big sombreros, frilly shirts, cowboy boots, and tight dark suits embroidered with silver. They sing romantic, sentimental songs accompanied by guitars and violins. In Mexico City, mariachi bands gather at Garibaldi Square, hoping to be hired by passersby. In Mexican tradition, suitors hire mariachis to serenade their lovers, husbands to serenade their wives. The most popular serenading hours are between two and four o'clock in the morning. Mariachis entertain at virtually all Mexican parties, weddings, and public fiestas.

DANCE

To the ancient Mexicans, dance was as important as music. Like music, dance was highly religious. The Aztecs and the Mayans danced to communicate with the gods and to bring good luck. They had dances at almost every occasion, such as marriage, war, hunting, and the harvest. To destroy Indian culture, the Spanish conquerors forbade community dancing, but their efforts failed in the end. Today the Institute of Fine Arts is home to the Ballet Folklórico, the national folkloric dance troupe.

The most beautiful and powerful Mexican dances are of pre-Spanish origin. The deer dance of the Yaqui Indians—the Yaqui Indian Stag Dance—is popular all over Mexico. Originally performed to attract luck in hunting, this dance is now performed at many religious fiestas and ceremonies. This exciting dance depicts the chase and kill of a deer, with all the dancers portraying animals with amazing realism. Another favorite is the Sandunga dance from Tehuantepec, famous for its beautiful music.

One of the few colorful dances introduced after the Spanish conquest is *los moros* (lohs MOH-ros), about the war between Moors and Christians in Spain. It is performed at bullfights and other celebrations. Half of the dancers dress as Moors, the other half as Christians. *Los moros* may be performed by as large a troupe as a thousand dancers but usually involves a group of about a dozen. It remains a popular ritual dance, especially around the Federal District and central states.

Probably the most spectacular of all traditional dances is the voladores *(vohl-AH-door-eh), or flying pole dance. It is an ancient rain dance that is still performed by the Náhuatl and Totonac Indians in several Mexican towns.*

Four men wearing feathered costumes are tightly secured by ropes to a pole standing 100 feet (30 m) tall. They represent the four seasons. Another man is seated on a small platform on top of the pole, playing an instrument. The four men with ropes drop off the pole and swing around 13 times before they reach the ground. The total number of rotations, which is 52, represents the number of weeks in a year.

The Mexican hat dance is a national folk dance that has become famous around the world. Dancers clap their hands and step on the rim of the hat as they circle it. Other colorful dances are the Zapotec feather dance from the state of Oaxaca and the Náhuatl quetzal dance from the city of Puebla. Quetzal dancers wear feathered headdresses and carry shields.

LITERATURE

Octavio Paz (1914—98) was a writer and poet noted for his elegant style, as well as his insight into and knowledge of Mexican society. One of his most famous works is *The Labyrinth of Solitude: Life and Thought in Mexico*. In this book he tried to analyze the Mexican character. In 1990 Paz became the first Mexican to receive the Nobel Prize in literature.

Murals by Diego Rivera symbolizing Mexican history deck the walls of the National Palace in Mexico City.

Other internationally recognized authors include Juan Rulfo (1917—86) and Amado Nervo (1870—1919). Carlos Fuentes (b. 1928) is Mexico's best-known contemporary writer. Two of his major novels, *The Death of Artemio Cruz* and *Where the Air Is Clear*, portray the social elite and the often seamy side of Mexican life and politics. Both these novels have been translated into numerous foreign languages. His 1985 novel *Gringo Viejo* became a best-seller in the United States and was filmed as *The Old Gringo* (1989), starring Gregory Peck and Jane Fonda.

A surprising number of well-known British and American authors have written about Mexico or set some of their best novels in Mexico, usually after having lived or traveled there. These authors include Saul Bellow, Ray Bradbury, Graham Greene, Jack Kerouac, D. H. Lawrence, Jack London, Katherine Anne Porter, Oscar Lewis, and John Steinbeck.

THE ART SCENE TODAY

The art scene in contemporary Mexico, in the tradition of its rich history, continues to nurture and produce a great number of artists. Unfortunately these artists are hardly known outside Mexico. Although there has been international recognition for Mexican muralists such as Diego Rivera, David

Siqueiros, and José Orozco, other contemporary artists such as José Fors, Manuel González Serrano, Alicia Rahon and Ricardo Martínez are largely unknown outside their home country. In spite of the many foreign styles that have influenced Mexican art over the years, indigenous Indian style continues to be the backbone of contemporary Mexican art, as shown in Mexican architecture, jewelry, fashion, and advertising.

INTERNET LINKS

www.mexicocity.com/

This website offers brief coverage of the highly impressive National Museum of Anthropology, with illustrations and links to many parts of the museum.

www.visitmexico.com/wb/Visitmexico/misiones_y_haciendas

This website covers the history of Mexico's colonial architecture, especially the five Franciscan Missions at Sierra Gorda, declared World Heritage Sites by UNESCO.

www.mexconnect.com/articles/1875-what-is-the-mariachi

This online article offers a description, photos, and video links of Mexico's famous mariachi music.

www.mexconnect.com/galleries/506-women-potters-of-san-marcos-tlapazola-oaxaca

This web page contains photographs of women potters of San Marcos Tlapazola, Oaxaca, making traditional earthenware.

www.mexconnect.com/galleries/488-yuriria-16th-century-convent-in-guanajuato

Exterior and interior photographs of a 16th-century convent resembling a medieval fortress are the subject of this web page.

CAFE LA CABAÑA

LEISURE

People enjoying a quiet day at a café.

11

I N MEXICO PEOPLE SPEND their leisure time with their relatives, visiting shopping malls, and enjoying their hobbies and pastimes. Social status as much as personal taste determines the types of pastimes and activities people do in their spare time.

The upper classes spend their leisure dining out, traveling, and playing sports at country clubs, much as the wealthy in other countries do. Wealthy Mexicans can easily fly to Houston, Los Angeles, or New York to visit friends or go shopping. Poor Mexicans, on the other hand, must work from dawn to dusk to make a living. For them, fiestas are the only leisure they can afford.

Mexican boys play a game of pogs in the plaza at Taxco, Guerrero.

The grand Plaza de Toros in Mexico City is the largest bullfighting arena in the world.

Sunday is the most leisurely day of the week for all Mexicans. It is an important family day. Favorite Sunday pastimes include picnics, family gatherings, going to bullfights, and in smaller towns, going on dates around the town square.

BULLFIGHT

Bullfighting was introduced to Mexico by the Spaniards shortly after the conquest. For the next 300 years of colonial rule, bullfights were held regularly in Mexico to commemorate religious and civic celebrations. Bullfighting is one of the country's most popular spectator activities. Bullfighting is legal in Mexico, and the bullfighting season lasts from October to April. Mexico City's bullfighting ring, the Plaza de Toros, seats up to 50,000 people. It is the largest bullfighting ring in the world and twice as large as most rings in Spain.

Bullfighting, while often called a sport, is really more of an art form. It challenges a matador to have control over his own fears, to overcome the bull's ferocity, and to satisfy the expectations of the crowd.

The object of a bullfight is for the matador to kill an untamed bull with a sword. He attempts to do this by following a ritual that has been developed over centuries. The matador is assisted by two mounted picadors and three banderilleros on foot.

The fight begins when the ring *presidente* (preh-see-DEN-tay) waves his handkerchief and the first bull rushes in. The average bull weighs about 1,100 pounds (500 kg). Sometimes dirt is thrown onto its back so that when it runs, the dirt flying off its back will show off the quickness of its movements.

A bullfight is divided into three parts called *tercios* (TEHR-see-ohs). The first *tercio* is called *puyazos* (poo-YAH-sohs), or stabs. Two picadors use lances to weaken the bull's shoulder muscles, causing its head to sag downward. This helps to expose the entry point for the sword's thrust. When the picadors leave the ring, the bull is raging but weakened. The second *tercio* involves the banderilleros, who sting the bull with lances and barbed sticks with brightly colored ribbons. The bull, bleeding profusely, is furious and begins to charge. In the final *tercio*, the matador has 16 minutes to kill the bull, or the fight is over. He attempts to do this by making daring passes at the bull with his cape,

The banderilleros lance the bull to weaken it before its final showdown with the matador.

or muleta, before thrusting his sword between the animal's shoulder blades into its heart.

OTHER SPORTS

Despite the popularity of bullfighting, the biggest spectator sport in Mexico is *fútbol* (FOOT-bohl), or soccer. The Azteca Stadium in Mexico City seats up to 114,000 people, more than twice as many as the Plaza de Toros bullfighting ring. The stadium is home to Mexico City's premier soccer team, América, and hosted the World Cup soccer final in 1970 and 1986. Matches are played in summer and fall, on Sunday afternoons and Thursday evenings. The Mexican national team has been one of the world's top 20 soccer teams since 1930 and was ranked 14th in the world in 2010. Mexico won the CONCACAF Gold Cup in 1993, 1996, 1998, 2003, and 2009, making it the champion of North and Central America.

Young boys play soccer in a junior-league game in Mexico City.

DIVERS OF ACAPULCO

The coastal resort of Acapulco is famous for its clavadistas (KEH-lav-ah-DEE-stahs), or cliff divers. These brave (or some might say foolhardy) young men plunge 115 feet (35 m) from the heights of the La Quebrada cliffs, timing their jump with the incoming waves. If they mistime their dive, there is not enough water to break their fall and stop them from hitting the rocky bottom. Getting back out of the water is also dangerous, since the tide can dash them against the rocks. Sometimes they dive at night, the scene eerily floodlit for the divers and the spectators. Divers often dive in groups or combinations from platforms at different levels.

Along the Pacific coast and in the southeast, including the Yucatán Peninsula, baseball is extremely popular. Children play in school and after-school leagues, and men play in parks and other open spaces. Mexico has two major baseball leagues.

Jai alai is a game of Spanish-Basque origin similar to handball. It is played by two or four persons on a three-wall court with a hard rubber ball the size of a golf ball. A player hurls the ball against the wall, and his opponent tries to catch it in his racket and return it. Jai alai is sometimes called *pelota vasca* (pay-LOH-tah VAS-kah), or Basque ball. Cockfighting, which is illegal in the United States, Canada, and many other countries, is another popular Mexican sport. These fights take place in an enclosed pit, usually outdoors. Spectators place bets on their favorite gamecocks. At the start of the fight, handlers hold the birds and allow them to peck at each other just out of range. When the birds become angry, they are released and allowed to engage in a full-out battle, until one is dead.

An owner provokes his bird at a cockfight. The Spanish brought the sport to the American continent.

A *charrería*, or rodeo, during a village festival. Besides attaining horse-manship skills, *charros* also learn to use the lasso.

CHARROS

Mexico's only truly national sport is perhaps the *charrería* (char-reh-REE-ah), which is similar to the American rodeo. The men who participate are called *charros* (CHAR-ros) and are considered some of the bravest, strongest men in Mexico.

The skills displayed during a *charrería*—roping, tying, riding, and branding cattle—were developed for use in cattle ranching. These skills also made the *charros* excellent cavalrymen in Mexico's various wars. The *charros* captured enemies and their cannons by lassoing them as if they were cattle.

After the Mexican Revolution, most large cattle ranches in Mexico were broken up by the government, and the glory days of the *charros* reached an end. To continue to compete and show off their skills, the *charros* started the *charrerías*. The biggest *charro* rings, known as *lienzo charros* (lee-EN-soh CHAR-ros), are in Mexico City and Guadalajara. Weekly competitions are held on Sundays.

At the start of the show, the horsemen ride around the ring to salute the judges and the public. The first event, called *cala de caballo* (KAH-lah day kah-BAL-yoh), is meant to demonstrate the rider's control over the horse. The rider guides his horse through a series of difficult maneuvers.

The second event is called the *coleadero* (koh-leh-ah-DAY-roh). The *charro* must grab a wild bull by the tail and roll it over on its back. Points are given for how quickly and neatly the *charro* completes this difficult task.

The remaining events involve bronco bucking, bull riding, and lassoing. Some of these events are the most exciting of the whole show. Women also compete in their own events at the *charrería*. Though they ride their horses sidesaddle as a mark of femininity, they are extremely skilled riders.

Charros give much thought to their clothing and often spend a lot of money on their outfits or on equipment for their horses. The typical *charro* dress includes embroidered shirts, serapes, and dark blue pantaloons embroidered in gold.

Male *charros* are famous ladies' men. They idolize women and can be very romantic, and their strength and bravery make them very attractive to women. They are also very devoted to their horses. There is an aura of nostalgia about the *charro*—the hero of a romantic era that is quickly vanishing from contemporary Mexican society.

INTERNET LINKS

www.sacharro.com

This website offers descriptions, pictures, and video links of a local *charros* organization.

www.mexconnect.com/galleries/498-skimboard-kids-on-a-mexican-beach

This web page provides spectacular action pictures of Mexican kids surfing on the Pacific coast.

www.bestday.com/Editorial/Corrida-de-toros/

This website offers a comprehensive account and pictures of a typical bullfight in the Plaza de Toros, the world's largest bullring.

www.mexexperience.com/guide/mexicophotos/acapulco.php

A collection of spectacular photographs showing divers jumping from the cliffs near Acapulco is provided in this website.

FESTIVALS

La Parroquia of San Miguel de Allende is decorated with colorful offerings during the Day of the Dead.

12

MEXICO CELEBRATES MORE
festivals than any other Latin American country. Even before the Spanish arrived, indigenous Mexicans held feasts to celebrate natural phenomena and religious rituals.

FIESTAS

Ancient Indian fiestas were mostly somber religious events. At some of the celebrations, the Indians ate human flesh they had offered as a sacrifice to the gods. Today, while some fiestas are solemn affairs meant to pay homage to a saint, a hero, or a tradition, many other fiestas are joyful, fun-filled events.

Female dancers performing with baskets of flowers for a festive event in Mexico.

Despite centuries of effort by the Spanish settlers to eradicate pagan rituals and replace them with Christian feasts, many of the original pagan holidays are still celebrated. On any day of the year, a fiesta is held in at least one town in Mexico.

Fiestas usually last one or two days, but if the patron saint is especially important, they can last up to a week. The Feria de San Marcos is celebrated in Aguascalientes for 10 days every year, starting on Saint Mark's Day on April 25. Festivities are usually held around the church and the main plaza, or *zócalo*, both of which are colorfully decorated. During the day, people crowd the open-air markets to buy candy, fruit, toys, and handicrafts. At night, festivities include folk dances, fireworks, and music. The festivities are usually paid for by someone chosen by the community. It is considered an honor to be chosen, and the sponsor gains the gratitude of the townspeople and a good reputation in the community.

Dance troupes from all parts of Mexico come together for the annual Independence Day Parade in San Miguel de Allende during September.

INDEPENDENCE DAY

The most important Mexican patriotic fiesta is on September 16, the anniversary of the day in 1810 when Father Miguel Hidalgo proclaimed Mexico's independence from Spain.

This annual celebration actually begins the evening of September 15 with a reenactment of Father Hidalgo's call to battle, called El Grito de Dolores. The ceremony takes place simultaneously throughout Mexico at 11 P.M. In an internationally televised live broadcast, the president of Mexico appears on the central balcony of the National Palace in Mexico City and repeats Father Hidalgo's rallying cry. A replica of the Dolores church bell used to call the battle is then rung, followed by the ringing of the Metropolitan Cathedral bells.

The *zócalo* below the president is filled with celebrating Mexicans, in the same way that Times Square in New York City is crowded on New Year's Eve. In every municipality in Mexico the same ceremony takes place, with the mayor coming out on the central balcony of the city or town hall, reciting El Grito and ringing a replica of the bell of Dolores. In Mexico City and the provinces, magnificent fireworks follow.

El Grito is also recited in the United States in cities where large communities of Mexican-Americans live. Mexican government officials are sent to cities such as Los Angeles, San Francisco, San Diego, Chicago, and New York City to recite the battle cry and give a speech in Spanish to city officials. Outside Mexico City, bullfights are staged, but this anniversary is usually dedicated to rest. Mexico celebrates the birth of José María Morelos, the hero of the war for independence, on September 30.

Families gather and decorate the cemetery to welcome back the souls of their loved ones as part of Day of the Dead celebrations. Food for the dead is also placed on a decorated table that includes a photograph of the deceased along with flowers and other offerings.

DAY OF THE DEAD

The Day of the Dead, the most important religious and Indian festival of the year in Mexico, is also one of the most peculiar of all Mexican fiestas. This celebration originated in Europe in the ninth century and was introduced in Mexico by the Spaniards. It blended with existing Aztec beliefs concerning death and departed spirits. Weeks before the event, markets and bakeries sell special breads baked in human form, skull-shape sweets, toy coffins, and papier-mâché skeletons. Flower markets overflow with marigolds, which in Aztec times were offered to the dead.

On October 31, villagers await the *muertitos chicos* (moo-ehr-TEE-tohs CHEE-kohs), or souls of dead children. Toy-shaped cakes, hot chocolate, and honey are offered to sweeten the visit of these souls to earth. Adult souls are believed to return the following night, November 1. Families prepare delicious traditional feasts for their arrival. The dead are believed to eat the "spirit" of the food. Often a candlelight vigil is kept in the town cemetery the night the souls are expected to arrive. Families gather on the graves of their departed to keep them company on their annual return. The next day, November 2, is the official Day of the Dead. Everyone celebrates by eating the offered food.

FEAST OF OUR LADY OF GUADALUPE

Every year on December 12, Mexicans honor the Virgin of Guadalupe to celebrate the day of her miraculous appearance to the Indian peasant Juan Diego. Millions make a pilgrimage to the Basílica de la Virgen to thank her for answered prayers. Many crawl up the hill on their hands and knees, hurting themselves as an act of penitence. In spite of these sacrifices, a festive atmosphere prevails around the church. Beginning the evening of December 11, the square in front of the basilica becomes a stage for a night of traditional song and dance. Because this feast is close to Christmas, many Christmas activities also take place. Although many smaller celebrations take place in churches throughout Mexico, the largest celebration is held at the shrine outside Mexico City. This shrine is visited by more pilgrims than any other Catholic site in the world, with the exception of the Vatican in Rome.

CALENDAR OF EVENTS

Mexican author Octavio Paz wrote that Mexico's poverty "... can be measured by the frequency and luxuriousness of our holidays. Wealthy countries have very few: there is neither the time nor the desire for them, and they are not necessary... But how could a poor Mexican live without the two or three annual fiestas that make up for his poverty and misery? Fiestas are our only luxury." In a typical year, Mexicans can celebrate up to 60 national and local holidays and religious festivals. Some of Mexico's more important holidays:

January 1	*New Year's Day*
February 5	*Constitution Day*
March 21	*Birthday of Benito Juárez*
March/April	*Good Friday*
March/April	*Easter Monday*
May 1	*Labor Day*
September 16	*Independence Day*
November 20	*Anniversary of the Mexican Revolution*
December 25	*Christmas*

The following are not national holidays but are widely observed and celebrated:

Late February	*Carnival*
Before Easter	*Holy Week*
May 5	*Cinco de Mayo/Anniversary of the Battle of Puebla in 1862*
May 10	*Mother's Day*
July 25	*Day of Saint James*
August 15	*Day of the Virgen de la Asunción*
August 25	*Day of San Luis*
September 1	*President's annual report to the nation*
October 12	*Día de la Raza (Day of Ethnicity)*
November 2	*Day of the Dead (All Soul's Day)*
November 22	*Day of Saint Cecilia*
December 12	*Feast of Our Lady of Guadalupe, patron saint of Mexico*

A piñata stall stocks up in time for Christmas celebrations.

THE CHRISTMAS SEASON

The Christmas season in Mexico is a combination of Spanish colonial customs and traditions picked up from the United States.

The posada, literally "inn," dates from colonial times, when missionaries tried to illustrate the Christmas story for their Indian converts. Beginning on December 16 and continuing every night through Christmas Eve, posadas reenact Joseph and Mary's search for lodging in Bethlehem. Processions move through the streets carrying lighted candles. At the door of a designated house, the group stops, sings traditional posada songs, and asks for lodging. After repeated rejections, the door is finally opened. The group joyfully enters, and the party begins.

Highlighting the posada are traditional food and drink, and for the children, the breaking of the piñata, a clay pot shaped like an animal or a carnival figure and covered with papier-mâché and ribbons. In most homes, piñatas are filled with candies and toys; some are filled with money. Blindfolded children take turns swinging a broomstick at the piñata, which hangs above them on a rope. When the piñata shatters, the children scramble for the gifts.

While some Mexican families have adopted the U.S. tradition of giving gifts on Christmas Day, Epiphany on January 6 is the traditional gift-giving day in Mexico. Epiphany is the day the three gift-bearing kings of the East visited the baby Jesus. Commemorating their arrival in Bethlehem, Mexican boys playing the part of the three kings wear fake beards, crowns, and long robes and sit in the plazas of towns where children go to have their pictures taken.

For Christmas parties, a special doughnut-shaped cake is baked with a small doll inside. Traditionally the guest who receives the slice of cake containing the doll must give a feast on February 2.

New Year's celebrations in Mexico used to be similar to Thanksgiving celebrations in the United States; they were traditionally quiet family affairs. Mexico's New Year has since become much like New Year's celebrations in the United States, with lively parties and festivities.

INTERNET LINKS

www.justmexico.org/mexico/mexico-festivals.asp

This website describes with photographs some of the main festivals celebrated in Mexico, including Carnival, the Day of the Dead, and Holy Week.

www.bbc.co.uk/news/world-latin-america-11322686

This BBC News web page features a colorful slideshow of photographs of Mexicans celebrating the bicentennial of Mexican independence in 2010.

www.facts-about-mexico.com/mexican-christmas.html

This article from the Facts-About-Mexico.com website explains the special characteristics of a Mexican Christmas.

www.mexconnect.com/galleries/112-chiapas-celebrates-the-day-of-the-dead

A gallery of photographs of this website shows the Day of the Dead celebration in Chiapas. For photos of the celebration in Oaxaca, visit www.mexconnect.com/galleries/93-day-of-the-dead-pictures-of-oaxaca.

www.sacred-destinations.com/mexico/mexico-city-basilica-guadalupe

This website offers the history and photographs of the Basilica of Our Lady of Guadalupe and a guide to the legend of the Lady of Guadalupe.

FOOD

Fresh vegetables sold at a market in Mexico.

13

M EXICAN CUISINE IS A MELTING pot of flavors, using ingredients and cooking methods from many countries. Spanish cuisine, incorporating some Arabian dishes, brought to Mexico onions, garlic, sugar, beef, pork, chicken, and cheese. Catholic nuns were among the first to mix local food products with those from Spain, creating a unique Mexican taste.

Mexican food is known for its variety, color, and spiciness, reflecting native influences as well as those of Spain, France, and South America.

Mexican sweets for sale at a confectionary stall in the city of Puebla.

No Mexican meal is complete without corn tortillas or tacos. These are sold in every restaurant and street stall in Mexico.

French cuisine was introduced in Mexico during the reign of Maximilian in the 1860s. Breads with that typically French crisp crust and many kinds of sweet rolls can be found everywhere in Mexico. Flan, an egg custard topped with a layer of caramel, is a French dessert that appears on the menus of almost every Mexican restaurant, both in Mexico and beyond.

Other European contributions to Mexican cuisine include sausages and beer from Germany and pasta from Italy. Spices and mangos arrived aboard ships from Asia. Hamburgers, doughnuts, pancakes, and pies from the United States are also becoming increasingly popular items on the Mexican menu.

Many foods consumed by people all over the world today originated in Mexico and were introduced to the rest of the world by Spanish conquistadores returning home in the 16th century. Corn is probably Mexico's greatest contribution to "international" cuisine; the country has also introduced tomatoes, chocolate, vanilla, various types of squash including pumpkins, peanuts, assorted beans, avocados, chilies, guava, coconuts, pineapples, papayas, and turkeys.

STAPLES: CORN TO TORTILLAS

Ancient Mexican civilizations introduced to the world two priceless foods: corn and chilies. Although many other foods are indigenous to Mexico, these two products remain the staples of the Mexican diet.

For thousands of years before Cortés arrived in Mexico, corn was the most important food of the indigenous population. The Indians called it *toconayo* (toh-koh-NAH-yoh), which means "our meat." They believed that the gods had molded humans from corn.

The Mexicans were known for a time as the "people of corn." All ancient Mexican civilizations devoted ceremonies to gods and goddesses of corn. Although religion in modern Mexico has discontinued this practice, Mexicans

Chili, an indigenous Mexican food, plays an important part in the country's cuisine. The Aztecs and the Mayans, who cultivated and consumed chili, created recipes that are still in use. These ancient peoples believed that chili had medicinal value, and modern nutritionists agree. A fresh chili is an excellent source of vitamin C and minerals. There are more than 100 types of chilis in Mexico, mostly because of climatic variations within the country. Each chili variety has its own flavor. Generally the smaller the chili, the hotter it is.

continue to revere this ancient food. For example, roadworkers clearing brush from the shoulders of the highway and groundskeepers in public parks rarely cut stalks of wild corn. As a result, it is not unusual to see corn growing in a downtown plaza or in the middle of a construction site.

No part of the corn plant goes unused. The young, tender ears and husks are used for tamales and *atole* (ah-TOH-lay), and the corn silk is made into a medicinal tea, said to be good for the kidneys. When dried, the kernels are used for masa, or tortilla dough; the husks for tamales; and the dried stalks for cattle feed. Corn is used in everything from popcorn to cornflakes. It is an ingredient in syrups, desserts, cornstarch, oil, grits, and coloring for caramel, dextrin, glucose flour, and beer as well as a feed for poultry and other livestock.

The most important use of corn is centuries old. Corn forms masa, the dough for tortillas and tamales. A Mexican table without tortillas is said to be an empty table, so cornmeal tortillas must be served with every meal. Corn is the basis of hundreds of dishes. The first cooking lesson a peasant's daughter learns is how to prepare the *nixtamal* (neex-tah-MAHL)—corn cooked in a solution of lime and water—for the next day's tortillas.

TRADITIONAL MEALS

Mexico's best-known traditional foods include tacos; enchiladas; tamales, cornmeal dough filled with meat and chili sauce and wrapped in cornhusks and steamed; quesadillas, grilled or fried tortillas stuffed with meat, cheese, potatoes, squash blossoms, or chilies; chalupas, tortillas fried and topped with meat and beans, chilies, tomatoes, and onions; gorditas, small, thick tortillas fried with chopped meat and vegetables, cheese, shredded lettuce, and chili sauce on top; and flautas, extra-long tacos.

Another famous Mexican dish is *chiles rellenos* (CHEE-lehs-reh-LYEH-nos). Tangy, delicious, long green peppers are stuffed with either cheese or ground meat, dipped in egg batter, fried, and then simmered in a bland tomato sauce.

For a two-month period beginning in mid-August, a special dish called *chile en nogada* (CHEE-lee en noh-GAH-dah) is served. The stuffing is often made from ground pork, and the chilies are decorated with sauce, seeds, and parsley to make the red, white, and green colors of the Mexican flag. This dish is served to celebrate Mexican Independence Day.

Mole pastes and powders being sold at the Merced Market in Mexico City. Mole is a very rich sauce made from more than 30 ingredients, all of which are ground or puréed. A good mole sauce takes two days to prepare.

TRADITIONAL DRINKS

Mexicans are great coffee drinkers, especially since high-quality coffee is grown in Mexico. Coffee is always served at the end of a meal, never before, as most Mexicans prefer not to drink coffee on an empty stomach. Because Mexican coffee is very strong, it is usually served with a lot of sugar. A popular coffee drink is *café con leche* (kah-FEH kon LAY-chay), a blend of strong black coffee and hot milk frequently served in a tall, thick glass.

Hot chocolate has been consumed in Mexico since pre-Spanish times. It is a favorite drink for modern Mexicans at both breakfast and supper. Mexicans drink hot chocolate with a touch of cinnamon, a custom dating back to the ancient Aztecs, who added honey and cinnamon instead of sugar. Not surprisingly, Mexicans also drink corn. Masa, the dough used to make tortillas, is the foundation for *atole*, a widely enjoyed beverage prepared by diluting masa in water and boiling it until it is as thick as a milkshake. Mexicans make a good number of alcoholic beverages from fruits or cacti. Tequila, mescal, and *pulque* (POOL-kay) are all made from the agave plant. Some drinks, such as tequila, are famous around the world.

Water flavored with fruit juice and syrups is very popular, while soft drinks are another favorite.

THE MEXICAN KITCHEN

While many kitchens in Mexico have modern utensils and appliances, such as blenders and food processors, many essential cooking tools used in modern Mexico were created thousands of years ago. Mexicans rely extensively on clay cookware, bowls, and pitchers. The following are some traditional Mexican cooking tools:

- **Bean masher** *This is usually made from wood.*
- **Molinillo** *This is a beautifully carved chocolate beater, usually made from wood.*
- **Comal** *This is a round, flat plate of tin or unglazed earthenware on which tortillas are cooked.*
- **Chiquihuite** *This is the traditional tortilla basket made from woven reed grass and lined with a cloth to keep the tortillas warm.*
- **Tortilla press** *This is used for rolling and shaping tortillas.*
- **Flan mold** *This three-piece tin utensil is used for cooking flan in a water bath.*

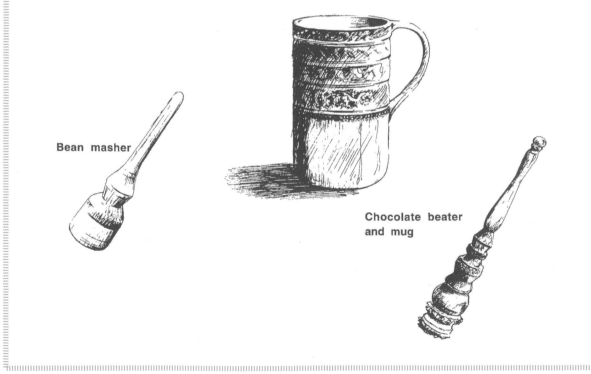

Bean masher

Chocolate beater and mug

- **Metate** *This is a sloping, rectangular piece of volcanic rock, supported on three stout legs. Together with a* metlapil, *or stone rolling pin, it is used for grinding corn, chilies, cacao, and other ingredients for making sauces.*

- **Molcajete *and* tejolate** *These are a mortar and a pestle made from porous, volcanic stone. They are used to grind spices and make sauces and are considered indispensable in a Mexican kitchen.*

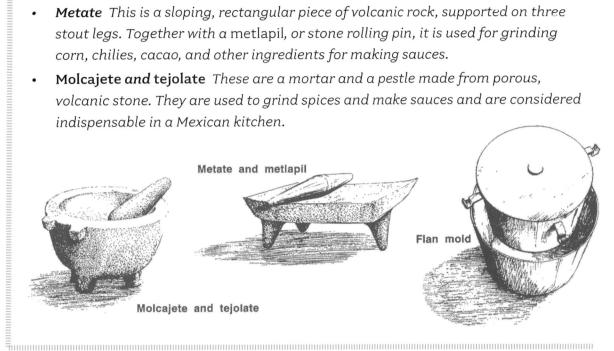

Metate and metlapil

Flan mold

Molcajete and tejolate

MARKETS AND FOOD STALLS

Mexicans shop daily at open markets for fresh food. There are temporary and permanent markets. They are the best places to go to for fresh fruit and vegetables. Bartering, or trading goods, is common and even expected in most marketplaces.

Tiendas (tee-EN-dahs) are small grocery stores. In some smaller towns and villages, these stores also serve as social centers. *Conasupos* (koh-nah-SOO-pohs) are government-owned stores originally designed to sell basic staples at controlled prices. The government dispatches mobile *conasupos*, usually large trucks or trailers, to remote areas of the country where no permanent stores are found. Prices are usually lower at *conasupos* than at other stores. Finally there are the *supermercados* (soo-per-mer-KAH-dos), which can vary from large *tiendas* to warehouse-size stores. Prices are usually high at the *supermercados*, but shoppers have a broader selection of products.

REFRIED BEAN DIP

This dish is delicious as a warm dip for corn or tortilla chips.

14.6-ounce (415-g) can spicy refried beans
1 chopped medium onion
8 ounces (227 g) sour cream
2 chopped tomatoes
4 to 8 ounces (113 to 227 g) grated cheddar cheese
1 bunch green onions, chopped

Heat beans and chopped onion in a pan, adding a little water to make the mixture smooth. Allow to cool. Spread bean mixture onto a large flat plate. Spread sour cream on beans. Sprinkle chopped tomatoes, cheese, and green onions on sour cream. Chill in refrigerator for one hour. Serve with chips or nachos.

Fondas (FOHN-dahs) are food stalls found in the markets that sell meals, including beans, rice, soup, and tortillas. Sidewalk stands, where fast food is sold, are also popular.

MEALTIMES

Mexicans start their mornings with a light breakfast, served between 6 and 8 A.M. The first meal of the day usually consists of coffee with tamales or a piece of bread or pastry. Brunch is a heartier meal. Eggs with meat or tortillas, accompanied by coffee and milk or fresh fruit juices, are served between 11 A.M. and noon.

The Mexican midday meal, *la comida*, is the heaviest and most traditional meal of the day. It is usually not served until around 2 or 3 P.M. The *comida* may include soup, rice or pasta, beans, tortillas or bread, dessert, and a fruit juice or beer. After lunch, except in major cities, nearly everything and everyone shuts down for the siesta.

Between 7 and 8 P.M., Mexicans enjoy their own form of English high tea called the *merienda* (may-ree-EN-dah). It consists of a cup of hot chocolate, coffee, or *atole* and some pastries and tamales.

Cena (SAY-nah), or dinner, is the third major meal of the day. It can be served anytime between 7.30 P.M. and midnight but is usually eaten between 9 and 10 P.M. It is lighter than the *comida* and might include leftovers from lunch, such as tacos or tortillas.

INTERNET LINKS

www.mexicanfood.about.com

This website offers vivid descriptions of ingredients and recipes with photographs.

www.mexicanfoodrecipes.org

This is a useful website offering dozens of recipes from almost every part of Mexico.

www.foodbycountry.com/Kazakhstan-to-South-Africa/Mexico.html

This website offers a history of Mexican cuisine, food festivals, and culinary customs, with some simple recipes.

www.mexconnect.com/articles/2255-calendar-of-mexican-food-festivals

This website provides a calendar of Mexico's food-based festivals, with descriptions.

www.allrecipes.com//Recipes/world-cuisine/latin-america/mexico/Main.aspx

This useful website provides simple instructions for cooking Mexico's top 20 recipes.

ZUCCHINI AND CORN CASSEROLE

This recipe serves four.

2 tablespoons (30 ml) butter or margarine

1 chopped large onion

1 green bell pepper, cored, seeded, and chopped

1½ pounds (700 g) sliced zucchini

2 cups (500 ml) frozen whole-kernel corn

2 large ripe tomatoes cut into chunks

2 medium tomatoes, chopped

4 tablespoons (60 ml) water

Salt and pepper

Preheat oven to 350°F (175°C). Melt butter or margarine in a Dutch oven or heavy pan over medium heat. Add onion and bell pepper, and cook for five to seven minutes, stirring until soft. Add zucchini. Stir until vegetables are coated with butter or margarine. Turn off heat. Add corn, tomatoes, water, and salt and pepper to taste. Stir vegetables using a long-handled wooden spoon. Cover the Dutch oven or pan and place in the oven. Cook for 20 minutes. Wearing oven mitts, remove the Dutch oven from the oven, and place it on the stovetop. Remove the lid and pierce the zucchini with a knife to check that it's tender. If it is not, place the lid back on the Dutch oven, return it to the oven, and cook for five minutes or more. Add more salt and pepper to taste if desired. Serve hot.

CHICKEN WITH MOLE SAUCE

This recipe serves four.

1 chicken, cut into 8 serving pieces

2 onions, quartered

4 cloves garlic, peeled and halved

6 sprigs each of fresh thyme, oregano, and parsley

12 small chilies

3 peeled ripe tomatoes

¼ cup (60 ml) sesame seeds

1 tablespoon (15 ml) dried oregano

1 clove

1 teaspoon (5 ml) ground allspice

¼ cup (60 ml) vegetable oil

8 cloves of garlic, peeled

1- to 2-inch (2.5- to 5-cm) piece of cinnamon stick

1 peeled and chopped plantain

1 ounce (30 g) unsweetened chocolate

Salt to taste

Place chicken in a stew pot and add one of the quartered onions, garlic, and fresh herbs. Cover with water and bring to a boil, then cover the pot and simmer for about 30 minutes until chicken is tender. Remove the stems from the chilies, cut in half lengthwise, and remove seeds. Toast chilies briefly in a hot skillet, but do not overcook. Place chilies in a small bowl, cover with hot water, and set aside. Place the peeled tomatoes in a blender and pulse a few times. Toast sesame seeds in the skillet and add to the blender along with dried oregano, clove, and allspice. Blend until smooth. Add oil to the skillet and fry the second quartered onion for about five minutes. Add garlic cloves and cinnamon stick, and fry for two to three minutes. Remove with a slotted spoon and put in the blender. Fry plantain for a few minutes, then add to the blender. Blend everything until smooth. Strain the sauce and return it to the skillet. Add chocolate and season with salt. Add two cups (500 ml) of the chicken broth to the skillet along with the stewed chicken pieces. Cook for another 20 to 25 minutes uncovered. The sauce should be fairly thick when served. Serve hot with rice or soft tortillas.

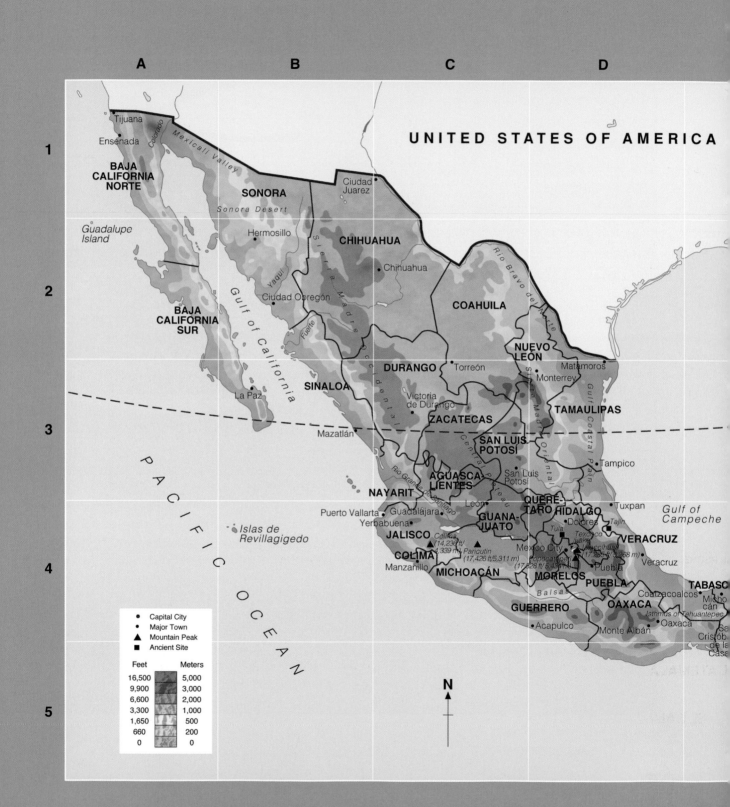

MAP OF MEXICO

F

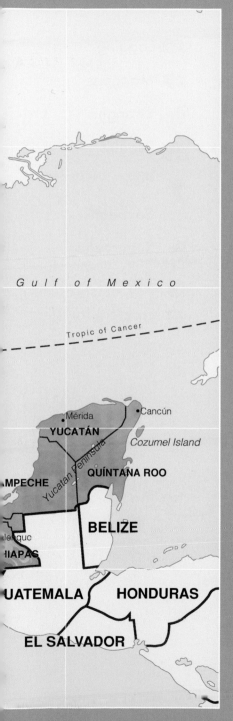

Acapulco, D4
Aguascalientes, C3—C4

Balsas River, C4, D4
Baja California Norte, A1—A2
Baja California Sur, A2—A3, B2— B3
Belize, F4

Campeche, E4, F4
Cancún, F3
Central Plateau, C3—C4
Chiapas, E4—E5
Chihuahua, B1—B2, C1—C2
Chihuahua (city), C2
Ciudad Juarez, C1
Ciudad Obregón, B2
Coahuila, C2—C3, D2
Coatzacoalcos, E4
Colima, C4
Colorado River, A1
Cozumel Island, F3—F4

Dolores, D4
Durango, B2—B3, C2—C3

Ensenada, A1

Fuerte River, B2

Guadalajara, C4
Guadalupe Island, A2
Guanajuato, C3—C4, D3
Guatemala, E4—E5, F4—F5
Gulf of California, B2—B3
Gulf of Campeche, D4, E4
Guerrero, C4, D4—D5

Hermosillo, B2
Hidalgo, D4

Islas de Revillagigedo, B4

Jalisco, C3—C4

La Paz, B3
León, C4

Manzanillo, C4
Matamoros, D3
Mazatlán, B3
Mérida, E3
Mexico City, D4
Mexican Valley, A1, B1
Michoacán, C4, D4
Monte Albán, D4
Monterrey, D3
Morelos, C4, D4
Mount Colima, C4
Mount Iztaccíhuatl, D4
Mount Paricutín, C4
Mount Popocatépetl, D4

Nayarit, C3—C4
Nuevo León, C2—C3, D2—D3

Oaxaca, D4—D5, E4—E5

Palenque, E4
Puebla, D4
Puerto Vallarta, C4

Querétaro, C4, D3—D4
Quintana Roo, F3—F4

Rio Bravo del Norte, C2, D2
Rio Grande de Santiago, C3—C4

San Cristóbal de las Casas, E4
San Luis Potosí, C3, D3
Sinaloa, B2—B3, C3
Sierra Madre Occidental, B2, C3
Sonora, A1, B1—B2
Sonora Desert, B1

Tabasco, E4
Tajín, D4
Tamaulipas, D2—D3
Tampico, D3
Texcoco Lake, D4
Tijuana, A1
Torreón, C3
Tropic of Cancer, A3, B3, C3, D3, E3, F3
Tula, D4
Tuxpan, D4

Veracruz, D3—D4, E4
Victoria de Durango, C3

Yaqui River, B1—B2
Yerbabuena, C4
Yucatán, E3—E4, F3—F4
Yucatán Peninsula, E3—E4, F3—F4

Zacatecas, C3

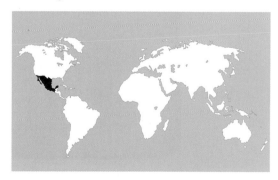

ECONOMIC MEXICO

Agriculture

- Bananas
- Coffee
- Cotton
- Farming
- Fishing
- Flowers
- Horses
- Livestock
- Logging
- Mangoes
- Oranges
- Peanuts
- Rice
- Soybeans
- Sugarcane
- Tobacco
- Tropical fruits

Manufacturing

- Car production
- Electronics
- Leather
- Manufacturing center
- Paper
- Seafood
- Steel
- Television
- Textiles

Services

- Airport
- Ports
- Tourism

Natural Resources

- Gold
- Oil

ABOUT THE ECONOMY

OVERVIEW

Mexico's free-market economy is made up of a combination of modern and traditional industry and agriculture. Mexico has doubled its trade with the United States and Canada since becoming a member of NAFTA in 1994 and enjoys free-trade agreements with more than 50 countries. Pension and fiscal reforms were passed in 2007 and were followed by an energy reform measure in 2008 and additional reforms in 2009. In spite of a better economy, Mexico still struggles with problems such as poverty, as income distribution remains highly unequal, the need to enhance the public education system, and the pressing importance to modernize infrastructure.

GROSS DOMESTIC PRODUCT (GDP)

$1.004 trillion (2010 estimate)

GDP per capita

$13,800 (2010 estimate)

GDP SECTORS

Agriculture: 4.2 percent
Industry: 33.3 percent
Services: 62.5 percent (2010 estimate)

CURRENCY

1 peso = 100 centavos
US$1 = 11.56 pesos (2011 estimate)

MAJOR EXPORTS

Manufactured goods, oil and oil products, silver, fruits, vegetables, coffee, cotton

MAJOR IMPORTS

Metalworking machines, steel-mill products, agricultural machinery, electrical equipment, car parts for assembly, repair parts for motor vehicles, aircraft, and aircraft parts

MAJOR TRADING PARTNERS

United States, China, Japan, South Korea, Germany

TOURISM

21.5 million tourists (2009 estimate)

WORKFORCE

Services: 62.9 percent
Industry: 23.4 percent
Agriculture: 13.7 percent (2005 estimate)

UNEMPLOYMENT RATE

5.6 percent (2010 estimate)

COMMUNICATIONS

Telephone lines: 19.425 million
Mobile cellular telephones: 83.528 million
Internet users: 31.02 million
Internet service provider accounts: 12.854 million (2010 estimate)

TRANSPORTATION

Airports: 1,819
Highways: 227,481 miles (366,095 km)
Railways: 10,884 miles (17,516 km)
(2010 estimate)

CULTURAL MEXICO

Caves in Sierra de San Francisco
Prehistoric rock paintings of people and animals painted high up on the walls and ceilings of several caves throughout Sierra de San Francisco.

Dolores Hidalgo
The town where Father Miguel Hidalgo y Costilla issued the "Cry of Dolores" for Mexican independence. The town boasts well-preserved historic buildings, such as the church from where Father Hidalgo issued the "cry," Father Hidalgo's home, and Independence Museum, formerly a prison.

San Miguel Huejotzingo Monastery
Located atop an ancient mound at the foot of Popocatépetl Volcano, the monastery is famous for its beautiful pieces of 16th-century art and architecture.

"Pyramid of the Niches"
Located in Tajín, Veracruz, the "pyramid of the 365 niches" was built by the Totonac civilization, a contemporary of the Maya civilization. Tajín is the Totonac god of thunder.

Chichén Itzá
One of the most spectacular of Mexico's ancient cities, Chichén Itzá was built by the Maya civilization. It includes the famous Castillo pyramid, the Caracol temple, the Ball Court, as well as many rock carvings of snakes and jaguars.

Basilica de la Virgen de Guadalupe
Church dedicated to the Virgin of Guadalupe. The blanket on which the image of the Virgin is said to be imprinted is enshrined inside the church.

Uxmal
Located in the midst of the tropical jungle, the ancient city of Uxmal was built by the Maya civilization. Its impressive structures include the Temple of the Magician pyramid, the House of the Turtles, the Ball Court, and the nunnery.

Teotihuacán
Perhaps the most famous of Mexico's ancient cities, the Toltec city of Teotihuacán, translated as "City of the Gods" from the Náhuatl language, includes the famous Pyramid of the Sun, the largest stone pyramid in pre-Columbian America. It measures 738 feet (225 m) on each side and is about 213 feet (65 m) tall.

Chapultepec Castle and Park
Castle and fortress built in the 18th century, it is home to the National Historical Museum. Inhabited by a succession of Mexican rulers, including Emperor Maximilian and his wife, Carlota, the castle was connected to Mexico City by a long avenue known today as Paseo de la Reforma.

Zócalo
Mexico City's main square is built upon the ruins of the ancient Aztec city of Tenochtitlán. It is the second-largest open square in the world, after Saint Peter's Square in the Vatican.

Monte Albán
Ancient city of the Zapotecs, a civilization that flourished in the central valley of Oaxaca from around 500 B.C. to A.D. 750. Main buildings in this city are the Great Plaza, the Ball Court, and a number of palaces and tombs.

OFFICIAL NAME
Estados Unidos Mexicanos (United Mexican States)

CAPITAL
Mexico City

DESCRIPTION OF FLAG
Three vertical bars of green, white, and red with a crest on the white panel of an eagle sitting on top of a cactus devouring a snake

NATIONAL ANTHEM
"Mexicanos, al Grito de Guerra" ("Mexicans, at the Cry of War")

AREA
Total: 3,287,612 square miles (8,514,877 square km)
Land: 3,266,199 square miles (8,459,417 square km)
Water: 2,108 square miles (5,460 square km)

ETHNIC GROUPS
Mestizo (Amerindian-Spanish) 60 percent, Amerindian or predominantly Amerindian 30 percent, white 9 percent, other 1 percent

POPULATION
113,724,226 (2011 estimate)

LIFE EXPECTANCY
Male: 73.65 years
Female: 79.43 years (2011 estimate)

BIRTHRATE
19.1 births/1,000 population (2011 estimate)

DEATH RATE
4.9 deaths/1,000 population (2011 estimate)

INFANT MORTALITY RATE
17.3 deaths/1,000 live births (2011 estimate)

LITERACY RATE
Male: 86.9 percent
Female: 85.3 percent (2005 estimate)

EDUCATION
Government expenditure on education: 4.8 percent of GDP
Daily newspaper circulation per 1,000 people: 94

LEADERS IN THE ARTS
Carlos Fuentes, Octavio Paz (literature), Frida Kahlo, Diego Rivera (fine arts)

POLITICS
System of government: constitutional republic
Current leader: Felipe Calderón (elected in 2006)
Next elections: 2012

TIME LINE

IN MEXICO	IN THE WORLD
300 B.C. Monte Albán civilization appears in southern Mexico.	
200 B.C. Teotihuacán civilization appears in central Mexico.	**116–17 B.C.** Roman Empire reaches its greatest extent, under Emperor Trajan.
A.D. 200 Mayan civilization appears in Yucatán Peninsula.	**600 A.D.** Height of Mayan civilization
1376 First Aztec king is crowned.	
1502–20 Reign of Aztec emperor Moctezuma II	
1519–21 Hernán Cortés conquers the Aztec Empire.	
1521–50 Spanish colonial administration is established.	**1530** Beginning of transatlantic slave trade organized by Portuguese in Africa
1550–1600 Ranching, industry, and mining expand.	**1558–1603** Reign of Elizabeth I of England
1600–1700 Colony suffers from economic stagnation and racial stratification.	
1700–1800 Bourbon monarchs in Spain revitalize the colony.	**1776** U.S. Declaration of Independence
1810 Miguel Hidalgo makes cry for independence.	
1821 Mexican independence is declared.	
1836 Texas becomes independent from Mexico.	
1846 Mexican–American War begins.	
1853 President Santa Ana sells additional territory, the Gadsden Purchase, to the United States.	
1858–61 Conflict over President Benito Juárez's reforms	**1861** U.S. Civil War begins.
1862–66 French intervention in Mexico	**1869** The Suez Canal is opened.
1910 Rebellion against Porfirio Díaz's rule	**1914** World War I begins.

IN MEXICO	IN THE WORLD
1917 Constitution is ratified.	
1927 Constitution of 1917 is amended to extend presidential term to six years.	
	1939 World War II begins.
1940 Mexico declares war on the Axis powers.	**1949** North Atlantic Treaty Organization (NATO) formed
1952–58 Women's suffrage is extended to the national level.	**1957** Russians launch Sputnik.
1970–76 Oil boom in Chiapas and Tabasco	**1986** Nuclear power disaster at Chernobyl in Ukraine
1992 NAFTA is signed by Mexico, Canada, and the United States.	
1994 Zapatista guerrilla movement begins in Chiapas.	**1997** Hong Kong is returned to China.
2000 Vicente Fox Quesada is elected president, ending 71 years of PRI-controlled government.	
2001 Congress passes a bill increasing the rights of indigenous people, but Zapatista leader Subcomandante Marcos rejects the bill	**2001** World population surpasses 6 billion; Terrorists crash planes into New York, Washington D.C., and Pennsylvania.
2002 Roberto Madrazo wins contest to lead the PRI.	**2004** Eleven Asia countries hit by giant tsunami, killing at least 225,000 people.
2006 PAN candidate Felipe Calderón is elected president.	
2008 Hundreds of thousands join marches throughout Mexico to protest against continuing wave of drug-related violence.	**2008** Earthquake in Sichuan, China, kills 67,000 people.
2009 Opposition PRI makes large gains in midterm congressional elections, winning 48 percent of seats in the chamber of deputies.	**2009** Outbreak of flu virus H1N1 around the world
2010 U.S. signs into law a $600 million bill to put more agents and equipment along the Mexican border to stem the flow of illegal immigrants.	**2011** Twin earthquake and tsunami disasters strike northeast Japan, leaving over 14,000 dead and thousands more missing.

GLOSSARY

atole (ah-TOH-lay)
A popular drink made from corn.

adobe
Sun-dried brick.

charrería (char-RER-EE-ah)
Mexican-style rodeo.

charros (CHAR-ros)
Mexican cowboys.

conquistadores
Spanish conquerors who colonized Mexico.

Creoles
People of Spanish descent born in Mexico.

ejidos (eh-HEE-dohs)
Communal farmlands.

encomienda (ehn-koh-mee-EHN-dah)
Spanish colonial system that granted Spanish settlers a large area of land in the American colonies in exchange for paying taxes to the Spanish king and converting the Amerindian population to Christianity.

haciendas
Large plantations.

machismo
Aggressive behavior by men that emphasizes masculinity.

mestizo
Person of mixed European and Indian ancestry.

peninsulares (pay-nin-soo-LAH-rehs)
Spaniards born in Spain but living in Mexico or other Spanish colonies in the Americas, usually representing the Spanish crown.

serape
A colorful shawl.

siesta
A nap taken after the main meal of the day, usually for one or two hours.

zócalo (ZOH-Kare-Loh)
A bandstand or platform in a central plaza or square, around which villages and cities are organized and which is the center of the town's activities; the main plaza in Mexico City is simply called the Zócalo.

FOR FURTHER INFORMATION

BOOKS

Gruber, Beth. *National Geographic Countries of the World: Mexico*. Washington, D.C.: National Geographic Children's Books, 2009.

Hoyt-Goldsmith, Jane. *Cinco de Mayo: Celebrating the Traditions of Mexico*. New York: Holiday House, 2010.

Hunter, Amy. *The History of Mexico* (Mexico—Beautiful Land, Diverse People). Broomall, PA: Mason Crest Publishers, 2008.

Williams, Colleen. *The Festivals of Mexico* (Mexico: Beautiful Land, Diverse People). Broomall, PA: Mason Crest Publishers, 2008.

MUSIC

El Trono de Mexico. *Famosas del Trono: Grandes Exitos*. Universal Latino, 2008.

Sones de Mexico Ensemble. *Fiesta Mexicana: Mexican Songs*. CD Baby, 2010.

Various artists. *Mexico and Mariachis: Music from and Inspired by Robert Rodriguez's El Mariachi Trilogy*. Milan Records, 2004.

BIBLIOGRAPHY

BOOKS

Beezley, William and Michael Meyer (eds.). *The Oxford History of Mexico*. New York: Oxford University Press, 2010.

Cramer, Mark. *Culture Shock! Mexico*. Portland, OR: Graphic Arts Center Publishing Co., 2002.

Fisher, John, Daniel Jacobs, Zora O'Neill, and Stephen Keeling. *Rough Guide to Mexico*, 8th ed. London: Rough Guides, 2010.

García-Oropeza, Guillermo, and Cristobal García Sánchez. *One Hundred and One Beautiful Small Towns in Mexico*. New York: Rizzoli, 2008.

Mavor, Guy. *Mexico—Culture Smart!: The Essential Guide to Customs and Culture*. London: Kuperard, 2006.

Noble, John, Kate Armstrong, Greg Benchwick, and Tim Bewer. *Lonely Planet Mexico*. Oakland, CA: Lonely Planet Publishing, 2008.

Reed, John. *Insurgent Mexico*. New York: International Publishers, 1988.

Spieler, Marlena. *Mexico* (Eyewitness Travel Guides). London: DK Travel, 2010.

Thomas, Hugh. *Conquest: Cortés, Montezuma, and the Fall of Old Mexico*. New York: Simon and Schuster, 1997.

Zohn, Ethan and David Rosenberg. *Soccer World: Mexico: Explore the World Through Soccer*. White River Junction, VT: Nomad Press, 2010.

WEBSITES

BBC News: Mexico Country Profile, http://news.bbc.co.uk/1/hi/world/americas/country_profiles/1205074.stm

CIA World Factbook: Mexico, https://www.cia.gov/library/publications/the-world-factbook/geos/mx.html

Global Exchange, www.globalexchange.org/campaigns/mexico/

MexConnect, www.mexconnect.com

Mexico Travel Guide, www.mexonline.com

The New York Times: Mexico, http://topics.nytimes.com/top/news/international/countriesandterritories/mexico/index.html

Visit Mexico, www.visitmexico.com

Wikipedia: Mexico, http://en.wikipedia.org/wiki/Mexico

World Travel Guide: Mexico, www.worldtravelguide.net/mexico

INDEX

INDEX